# INFORMATION LITERACY AND WRITING STUDIES IN CONVERSATION: REENVISIONING LIBRARY-WRITING PROGRAM CONNECTIONS

# INFORMATION LITERACY AND WRITING STUDIES IN CONVERSATION: REENVISIONING LIBRARY-WRITING PROGRAM CONNECTIONS

Andrea Baer

LIBRARY JUICE PRESS
SACRAMENTO, CA

Published in 2016 by Library Juice Press

Library Juice Press
PO Box 188784
Sacramento, CA 95822

http://libraryjuicepress.com/

This book is printed on acid-free, sustainably-sourced paper.

Library of Congress Cataloging-in-Publication Data
Forthcoming

# Contents

# Preface and Acknowledgements

While this book project has been a largely intellectual endeavor, it is also a personal one. It can be traced back to my earlier experiences in teaching college writing and literature while, in a previous incarnation, completing a doctoral degree in comparative literature. At the time I had no idea that it would ultimately lead me to libraries and to looking at the connections between the work of librarians and writing instructors. I think it was a happy accident. My interactions in both composition and library classrooms have greatly informed my work as a teacher, a librarian, and a scholar, and I am excited to see the work of compositionists and instruction librarians increasingly intersecting and opening up new possibilities for teaching and learning. My work as a librarian has also shaped my perspectives on undergraduate education and curriculum (recurring topics of this book), particularly since much of my library work has largely centered on building library instructional programming and partnerships that facilitate information literacy integration across the disciplines. Relatedly, the ideas from this book have been enriched by the interactions I have been honored to have with librarian colleagues in professional development workshops centered on teaching and learning, and in collaborating with faculty.

This book is most obviously about the powerful connections between teaching writing and information literacy. But just as importantly, it is also about connections between individuals and professional communities, and about how those connections can be nurtured and sustained. The foundations for such relationships are mutual listening and dialogue, and this book would not have been possible without such conversations. Though I appear as the sole author of this book and speak primarily from my own perspective, it is the result of many conversations and of the work and ideas of many.

I would like to give particular thanks to the compositionists and librarians who agreed to be interviewed about their collaborative experiences, which are the focal point of Chapter 4: Michelle Albertson, Dan DeSanto, Teresa Grettano, Susanmarie Harrington, Wendy Hayden, Stephanie Margolin, Caroline Sinkinson, and Donna Witek. Their openness and generosity has enabled a much fuller exploration in this book of the many possibilities for meaningful and creative library-writing program partnerships. Their thoughtful feedback during the writing of Chapter 4 has furthermore deepened the thinking that went into all of this book's chapters. Many thanks also to Bob Schroeder, who in sharing his own interviewing experiences for his book *Critical Journeys: How 14 Librarians Came to Embrace Critical Practice*, helped me to develop my approach to this publication's Chapter 4.[1]

I am also incredibly fortunate for the supportive colleagues and friends who provided their honest and thoughtful feedback and perspectives during my writing process: in particular Maria Accardi, Heidi L.M. Jacobs, and Catherine Minter. Their fresh perspectives have made this a much clearer and more thoughtful work, at the same time that their encouragement has helped me to push through moments of feeling stuck and of questioning whether I had anything new that was worth saying and being heard. My parents and friends have similarly offered their continual support, including listening when I talked through ideas that weren't yet crystallized. I also wish to express my gratitude to the Indiana University Libraries and my colleagues there for their support during the majority of my writing process, as well as the University of West Georgia Ingram Library and colleagues during the final stages of

---

1. Robert Schroeder, *Critical Journeys: How 14 Librarians Came to Embrace Critical Practice* (Sacramento, CA: Library Juice Press, 2014).

this book project. This book would not have been possible without their financial and moral support. I am furthermore grateful to everyone at Library Juice Press, in particular Rory Litwin and Alison Lewis, who have managed the copyediting, production, distribution, and marketing of this book, and have done so in a way that makes this work accessible.

# *Chapter 1*

## INTRODUCTION

In 2003 and 2004, rhetorician Rolf Norgaard wrote of "writing information literacy" in a two-part editorial published in the library professional journal *Reference and User Services Quarterly*.[1] A pedagogy for "writing information literacy," Norgaard argued, would situate research and information use within specific rhetorical and writing contexts. To cultivate such an approach, Norgaard called for building fuller partnerships among librarians and writing instructors.

The phrase "writing information literacy" was intended to convey the intertwined acts of writing, research, and information use.[2] Librarians' and writing instructors' pedagogies, when conceived of through this integrative lens, would enable information literacy education to function "as a means for asking better and better questions and for

---

1. Rolf Norgaard, "Writing Information Literacy: Contributions to a Concept," *Reference & User Services Quarterly* 43, no. 2 (Winter 2003): 124–30; Rolf Norgaard, "Writing Information Literacy in the Classroom: Pedagogical Enactments and Implications," *Reference User Services Quarterly* 43, no. 3 (2004): 220–26.

2. "Information literacy" has been defined most often as the ability to "recognize when information is needed and have the ability to locate, evaluate, and use effectively the needed information" (American Library Association, "Presidential Committee on Information Literacy: Final Report," January 10, 1989, http://www.ala.org/acrl/publications/whitepapers/presidential.). Though the library profession has probably been the most vocal advocate of "information literacy" education and though the term has often been viewed to connote simply instruction about library resources, the concept of information literacy encompasses much more, including the use of information for a wide range of purposes and contexts, and awareness of the social, cultural, and ethical dimensions of information creation, access, and use.

finding ever more persuasive lines of reasoning, and not just as a way to cite factoids and ready answers."[3] For Norgaard, "writing information literacy" would lead "to a more situated, process-oriented, and relevant literacy," as both professions worked together for pedagogical reform that would extend beyond these two fields.[4] Such an approach would contrast the artificial separation of writing and library research that has characterized much of both librarians' and compositionists' instruction.

Norgaard, of course, was not the first to draw attention to the need for greater collaboration among writing instructors and librarians, though he was probably the first individual from the field of composition and rhetoric to do so to a sizable audience. It remains nonetheless notable that he was writing in a library journal that compositionists were unlikely to read. The connections between writing and source-based research have been evident to many college writing instructors and librarians—though perhaps in varying ways—since the early developments of both writing and library instruction. (In fact, as early as 1952 an argument similar to Norgaard's was made by Haskell M. Block and Sidney Mattis in their *College English* article "The Research Paper: A Co-Operative Approach).[5] The intersections between writing and library instruction have been reflected in collaborations among individuals in our professions over the decades, as well as in the growing body of literature on integrated approaches to teaching writing and information literacy.[6]

---

3. Norgaard, "Writing Information Literacy in the Classroom," 222.

4. Ibid., 225.

5. Haskell M. Block and Sidney Mattis, "The Research Paper: A Co-Operative Approach," *College English* 13, no. 4 (1952): 212–15.

6. A number of librarians have given particular attention to the development of collaborations between librarians and writing instructors over time. See for example: M. Mounce, "Academic Librarian and English Composition Instructor Collaboration: A Selective Annotated Bibliography 1998-2007," *Reference Services Review* 37, no. 1 (2009): 44–53, doi:10.1108/00907320910934986; Grace L. Veach, "Tracing Boundaries, Effacing Boundaries: Information Literacy as an Academic Discipline" (Dissertation, University of Southern Florida, 2012), http://scholarcommons.usf.edu/cgi/viewcontent.cgi?article=5609&context=etd; Gail S. Corso, Sandra Weiss, and Tiffany McGregor, "Information Literacy: A Story of Collaboration and Cooperation between the Writing Program Coordinator and Colleagues 2003-2010" (National Conference of the Council of Writing Program Administrators, Philadelphia, PA, 2010).

The form and depth of such library-writing program alliances have varied considerably, ranging from the single librarian visit to fully re-envisioned courses that involve collaborative curricular development and co-teaching. Library-writing program partnerships, moreover, have extended beyond traditional classroom settings and are now also evident in alternative learning spaces such as writing centers and media labs.

Such collaborations illustrate that both writing and information seeking and use (information literacy) share powerful connections: both are central to posing and exploring problems and questions and to seeking informed and creative approaches to answering them. Writing and information literacy instruction invite students to analyze information sources, to reflect on varying perspectives on issues, and ultimately to contribute their own ideas about the questions they explore. Thus, at the heart of writing and information seeking and use are inquiry and critical thinking, which many college educators across disciplines view to be at the center of learning. The analytical and generative thinking that writing and information practices require—and the ways that these recursive processes repeatedly intersect—reflect the rich potential for teaching them as creative and interrelated acts of meaning making. Many in the fields of writing and library and information studies would likely agree with the educational reformer John Dewey's statement that "[o]nly by wrestling with the conditions of the problem at first hand, seeking and finding his own way out, does [the student] think."[7] As John Bean, a leader of the Writing Across the Curriculum movement, states when reflecting on Dewey's statement, "Part of the difficulty of teaching critical thinking, therefore, is awakening students to the existence of problems all around them."[8]

This awakening to and engagement in real-world problems is ideally what writing and information literacy instruction both center on. Scholarship on inquiry-based learning and critical pedagogy, much of which informs our (compositionists' and librarians') pedagogical practices

7. John Dewey, *Democracy and Education* (New York: Macmillan, 1916), 188.

8. John C. Bean, *Engaging Ideas: The Professor's Guide to Integrating Writing, Critical Thinking, and Active Learning in the Classroom*, 2nd ed, The Jossey-Bass Higher and Adult Education Series (San Francisco: Jossey-Bass, 2011), 3.

and much of which has been developed by individuals in our fields, has provided fertile ground for growth in our individual and collaborative teaching, as well as for curricular initiatives that extend beyond our two fields. Though writing instructors and librarians may often approach inquiry from different angles (for example, information literacy instruction tends to focus heavily on locating sources, while writing classrooms generally give more attention to textual analysis and construction of an argument that is supported by evidence from sources), we generally share the view that problem-posing and inquiry are key to meaningful and engaged learning. The varying approaches we have to encouraging critical inquiry have great potential to function in complementary and enriching ways, as is explored throughout this book.

## Common Disjunctures

The value of partnerships between English composition programs and libraries may seem obvious to many, given the importance in academic writing and in many writing classes of supporting one's ideas with sources and developing and articulating questions that are informed by source-based research. Both writing and source-based research are highly recursive processes that ideally begin with curiosity about a problem or question, which an individual then explores through an iterative process of information gathering, analysis, reflection, and ultimately communication about the relationship between one's own ideas and those presented by others. But despite these intersections, there is still a strong tendency for writing and library instruction to be taught in relative separation, with the latter frequently being viewed as a course "add-on." Similarly, conversations about writing and information literacy pedagogy have tended to exist in professional silos.[9]

---

9. See for example: Veach, "Tracing Boundaries, Effacing Boundaries: Information Literacy as an Academic Discipline"; Celia Rabinowitz, "Working in a Vacuum: A Study of the Literature of Student Research and Writing," *Research Strategies* 17, no. 4 (January 4, 2000): 337–46, doi:10.1016/S0734-3310(01)00052-0; Norgaard, "Writing Information Literacy in the Classroom"; Melissa Bowles-Terry, Erin Davis, and Wendy Holliday, "'Writing Information Literacy Revisited: Application of Theory to Practice in the Classroom," *Reference & User Services Quarterly* 49, no. 3 (2010): 225–30.

The one-off model of library instruction that is still the norm in many respects reinforces this. The tradition of the stand-alone library session implies that a short introduction to library resources should prepare students for a fairly straightforward task called academic research. Most library instruction for writing courses still uses this model, helping to keep intact a perception of information literacy as being simply about search mechanics. Norgaard's description in 2003 of writing instructor-librarian relationships still appears relevant today:

> On virtually every college campus librarians and writing teachers can point to each other as classroom colleagues and curricular compatriots. Yet the conversation is often limited to this level—and thus dismissed as a matter of local lore and personal friendship. Our collegial relations tend not to be sustained by a broader, theoretically informed conversation between writing and information literacy as disciplines and fields of endeavor.[10]

The reasons for this tendency toward separate dialogues are, of course, complex and multiple. They include differences in the historical developments of our fields, the professional training and education that prepares us for our work, the disciplinary discourses that inform much of that work, the structure of our workdays and our professional responsibilities, and the cultures and structural conditions of our institutions. Differences in librarians' and compositionists' everyday work environments and responsibilities are particularly significant, as these circumstances inevitably affect the nature of our interactions with students and other educators, as well as our common and differing perspectives on how students engage in seeking and using sources.

A number of librarians and compositionists have explored how views of information literacy and research instruction may generally differ between librarians and compositionists. Librarian Sheril Hook describes frequently differing perspectives of librarians and writing instructors (including those in writing centers) as follows:

---

10. Norgaard, "Writing Information Literacy: Contributions to a Concept," 124–125.

Currently, writing professionals tend to assume that the research process is subordinate to the writing process and thus have not given enough attention to understanding the research process itself and teaching it to students. Teaching librarians have tended to under-estimate or ignore the necessity to understand the writing process well enough to successfully integrate the research process with the formal teaching or tutorial of writing. And perhaps they also have tended to think of the writing process as subsequent to the research process.[11]

Hook argues for further dialogue and collaboration between librarians and writing professionals at the same time that she asserts a need for recognizing and appreciating distinctions between writing and research and between the work of librarians and writing educators.

Arguing along similar lines, librarian and library administrator Craig Gibson has noted the frequent disconnects between the teaching of writing and library instruction, which exist despite the vital connections between them. A major source of this problem, Gibson believes, lies in the view of library research as primarily a matter of search mechanics. He notes that writing instructors may sometimes view the use of library resources as more straightforward than the process actually is.

Writing teachers sometimes assume that learning to use the library is only a matter of hands-on practice, emphasizing narrow procedural skills [...]. Although hands-on work with tools is essential for students to gain confidence with information systems, an overemphasis on this particular kind of skill, removed from a larger rhetorical or critical-thinking context, shortchanges real learning of the type many librarians have been espousing in recent years.[12]

---

11. Sheril Hook, "Teaching Librarians and Writing Center Professionals in Collaboration: Complementary Practices," in *Centers for Learning: Writing Centers and Libraries in Collaboration*, ed. James K. Elmborg and Sheril Hook, Publications in Librarianship: No. 58 (Chicago: Association of College and Research Libraries, 2005), 21.

12. Craig Gibson, "Research Skills across the Curriculum: Connections with Writing-Across-the-Curriculum," in *Writing-Across-the-Curriculum and the Academic Library: A Guide for Librarians, Instructors, and Writing Program Directors*, ed. Jean (ed.) Sheridan, Thomas G., Jr. (fwd.) Kirk, and Elaine P. (afterword) Maimon, xix, 240 pp. vols. (Westport, CT: Greenwood, 1995), 55–69.

Gibson's observation would seem in keeping with that of compositionist James Purdy, who asserts that in many writing courses

> Research is typically addressed in a separate unit, positioned at the end of the course or sequence of courses. [...] Students are instructed to march through linear processes that compartmentalize research and writing: formulate a thesis, find (ideally print) sources to support that thesis, write a paper.[13]

The perception of library instruction as merely mechanical is reflected in the most common approach to library instruction: the "one-shot" library session. Because the one-shot is so limited in time, but is often the only time in which students are expected to learn "how to use the library" and how to do source-based research, these class sessions most often focus on the bare essentials of locating sources, leaving little time for considering the rhetorical purposes and contexts of research. Though librarians have increasingly been using individual library sessions to focus on other aspects of information literacy, such as source evaluation and integration of sources into one's writing, taking such an approach can be challenging when course instructors place a higher priority on librarians' teaching search mechanics.

One-shot sessions often imply that locating and using sources are distinct activities and that one can understand the essentials of academic research outside of a rhetorical framework. Although many librarians and writing instructors will agree that this strategy is not ideal, it has remained the most common practice for decades. (Among the top reasons given for this are time constraints and the difficulty of building meaningful teaching partnerships.)

At the same time that information literacy instruction continues most often to take the form of stand-alone class sessions, both librarians and compositionists know from their own writing and research experiences that these processes are closely interlinked. The library database search, often approached in library sessions as a matter of procedure, if done

---

13. James P. Purdy, "The Changing Space of Research: Web 2.0 and the Integration of Research and Writing Environments," *Computers and Composition* 27, no. 1 (2010): 48.

well actually requires complex analytical skills, such as identifying themes and patterns in research on a given topic and formulating and refining research questions with an awareness of the existing discourse. Such critical thinking ideally occurs throughout every step of the research process, including during the selection of a research tools, identification of effective search terms, evaluation of search results, initial selection of sources, and integration and analysis of sources.

But the same factors that contribute to an artificial separation between the teaching of writing and of information literacy, and to limited understandings of one another's professions and pedagogies, also point to ways that librarians and compositionists' expertise and pedagogies can function in complementary ways, with both parties learning from one another's unique experiences and expertise. Increased dialogue about our pedagogical work can help librarians and compositionists recognize the common experiences and challenges of our professions that can be sources of solidarity, helping us to generate creative responses to the pedagogical challenges of "writing information literacy."

Thus far I have discussed the common conception of "library instruction as procedural" as a significant obstacle to building meaningful library-writing program partnerships. Interestingly, this same barrier also reflects a shared experience and frustration of librarians and compositionists. Compositionists have similarly struggled with conceptions of writing as a mechanical and simple skill (that is, as an activity reduced to grammatical and syntax errors that are easily corrected and mastered). In reality, of course, composition and information literacy both involve complex abilities that are highly contextual and that develop over extensive periods of time.

## Converging Conversations

The interconnectedness of writing and research, as well as the similar experiences and challenges that compositionists and librarians have faced in conveying to other educators the complexity and significance of writing and information literacy education, present natural openings for meaningful partnerships across our professions. This is evident in many recent and current collaborations between individuals in both fields, as well as in a notable amount of scholarly literature on information literacy and English composition. The potential for collaboration seems especially great now, as library instruction programs are increasingly placing a strong emphasis on the rhetorical dimensions of research, and as library instruction becomes more deeply informed by pedagogical and process-oriented theories that align with many writing pedagogies. The progressively more complex role that technology plays in how people digest, share, and create information further suggests the importance of teaching writing and information literacy as interconnected processes and as integral parts of college curricula. Not only are Norgaard's comments in 2003 that "writing information literacy" enables "a more situated, process-oriented, and relevant literacy" still relevant today, but they have also taken on new resonance as the range of contexts and environments in which students compose and in which they engage with a wide range of information sources and formats have expanded.[14]

Moreover, with the growing attention in higher education to active and constructivist pedagogical approaches to learning, the opportunities for librarians and compositionists to join in their curricular efforts to support writing and information literacy education across the disciplines appear particularly significant now. There is clearly much that can be done in this area. Despite the significant progress both of our fields have made in communicating how writing and information literacy are central to higher-order thinking and the communication of complex ideas, librarians still struggle with the common misperception that information literacy and "library skills" can be boiled down to point-and-click skills, and writing instructors still grapple with the view of freshmen composition as a remedial course. And despite the powerful connections between writing and information practices, library and writing instruction tend to be presented largely in separation from one another.

---

14. Norgaard, "Writing Information Literacy in the Classroom," 225.

Although the reasons that potentially rich partnerships often do not form are complex, and although there are no easy solutions to strengthening our connections, dialogue across our professions has begun to expand at what appears an unprecedented pace, particularly as librarians become more vocal about the need for information literacy to be an integral part of college education, and as librarians expand their engagement with learning theories and conceptual frameworks for information literacy. This shift is evident in numerous conversations among academic teaching librarians and writing instructors about instruction, including those about the intersections between the recently adopted ACRL *Framework for Information Literacy for Higher Education* and the WPA *Framework for Success in Postsecondary Writing*, both of which take a holistic and inquiry-based approach to teaching writing and information literacy as abilities that are relevant in a wide range of rhetorical situations, and in both analog and digital environments.[15] The increasing conversations between our fields are further evident in a significant number of recent conference presentations, professional events, and calls for publication submissions concerning writing-information literacy connections.

This book is intended to help widen and deepen those conversations, as librarians and compositionists develop better understandings of the intersections between our work, as well as the barriers that sometimes stand between partnership. While the literature on the relationships between writing and information literacy and on library-writing partnerships continues to grow, this scholarship still remains limited and tends to focus most often on specific case studies. There have been few extensive explorations of the relationship between librarians' and compositionists' teaching, and still fewer that carefully consider the work of librarians and writing instructors not only in relation to research on student learning, but also in light of sociohistorical and structural contexts of library and

---

15. Council of Writing Program Administrators, National Council of Teachers of English, and National Writing Project, *Framework for Success in Postsecondary Writing*, 2011, http://wpacouncil.org/files/framework-for-success-postsecondary-writing.pdf; Association of College and Research Libraries, *Framework for Information Literacy for Higher Education*, 2015, http://www.ala.org/acrl/standards/ilframework.

writing instruction. This book seeks to do both. It does so with the view that through learning more about one another's pedagogical work and perspectives, compositionists and instruction librarians can deepen our understandings of both fields and, by extension, of pedagogical practices. With fuller understandings of our professions and of our educational roles, we can ultimately expand such teaching partnerships beyond our two professions, as we approach writing and information literacy education as shared responsibilities of all educators. Given the larger goals and the scope of this book, I do not provide a comprehensive discussion of the many collaborations that have occurred between individuals in these two professions, nor do I suggest a single strategy for approaching library-writing program partnerships. Working from the view that any collaboration depends greatly on context, I discuss concepts and general approaches that can help to inform library and writing instructors' individual and shared teaching, rather than suggesting a particular approach for all partnerships. Chapter 4's discussion of four specific librarian-compositionist collaborations also offers concrete examples of various shapes that partnerships might take. In the closing chapter I offer several general recommendations for strengthening connections between our professions.

## Chapters Overview

This introductory Chapter 1 has offered an overview of the interconnections between writing and information literacy, the disconnects that often prevent fuller dialogue, and the evolving role of writing-library teaching collaborations. These will remain the broader themes that structure this book, as I look more closely at the possibilities for and obstacles to collaboration from several angles.

Chapter 2, "Students as Writers and Researchers: Empirical Studies and Pedagogical Implications," provides a fuller view of what we know about how students engage with writing, information seeking, and information use, and how this can inform compositionists' and librarians' teaching practices. This scholarship, conducted primarily by compositionists and librarians, reflects how critical inquiry and knowledge creation are at the heart of both composing and information practices. Relatedly, these studies illustrate the highly contextual and social nature of writing and information practices and the long-term and gradual nature of writing and information literacy development. In providing fuller understandings of how students engage with and sometimes struggle with writing and information practices, such research suggests ways that compositionists and librarians can further support students in approaching writing and information use as personally meaningful processes with larger communicative and social functions. Chapter 2 further considers the importance of learning transfer for writing and information literacy education. Studies on transfer (the ability to apply knowledge and skills developed in one situation to a different context) provide insight into how writing and information practices can be taught as context-dependent activities, including through giving explicit attention to conceptual understandings of writing and information, dispositions related to writing and information processes, and metacognitive thinking.

The pedagogical implications of the empirical studies discussed in Chapter 2 are further explored in Chapter 3, specifically through the lens of two professional documents that have been particularly influential for many compositionists and librarians: the WPA *Framework for Success in Postsecondary Writing* and the ACRL *Framework for Information Literacy for Higher Education.*[16] This section explores intersecting themes of these frameworks, such as their representations of inquiry and knowledge creation as social and situated activities, and how these commonalities can serve as catalysts for expanding dialogue between our professions. The frameworks' pedagogical implications are also explored and related to what we know about students' writing and information literacy development. More specifically, I consider how the WPA and ACRL frameworks' stress on critical habits of mind and conceptual understandings related

---

16. Council of Writing Program Administrators, National Council of Teachers of English, and National Writing Project, WPA *Framework*; Association of College and Research Libraries, *Framework*.

to composing and information practices suggest strategies for teaching for transfer.

Chapter 4, "Composition-Library Collaborations: Notes from the Fields," shifts the focus from a more conceptual discussion of writing and information literacy pedagogy to four specific examples of close partnerships between compositionists and librarians. This section is primarily informed by my interviews with compositionists and librarians involved in extensive collaborations that are founded on an understanding of writing and information literacy as intertwined. The interviewees' creative approaches to "writing information literacy" illustrate the rich potential of joining efforts. Their collaborative experiences offer insight into common qualities of meaningful partnerships and into the conditions that help to cultivate and sustain them. At the same time the difficulties interviewees have experienced in expanding their collective efforts point to barriers that deserve further attention. These challenges frequently mirror structural and institutional barriers that prevent fuller cross-professional dialogue.

The interviewees' experiences and perspectives reflect constructive responses to many of these structural barriers (responses that include growing community through open dialogue; sharing experiences, perspectives, and instructional approaches; and examining factors and conditions that often prevent fuller conversations). Addressing such concerns, however, ultimately requires the engagement of a much larger number of individuals in our professions. In Chapter 5, "Expanding the Potential for Collaborations: Intersections between the Interpersonal and the Sociostructural," I look more closely at factors that often stand in the way of partnerships and ways we might address those challenges. Here I begin with reflection on the shared origins of writing and information literacy in literacy education and the ways that this history has influenced compositionists' and librarians' instructional and institutional roles in similar and distinct ways. With a larger view of the structural contexts in which compositionists and librarians work and how they have been influenced by a longer history, I then revisit the possibilities for library-writing partnerships and common barriers to them. Reviewing sociological and psychological research on librarian-faculty relations, I reflect on institutional structures and conditions that often support or prevent the development of partnerships. I also consider how this scholarship might help inform our shared efforts to advocate for writing and information literacy education as the shared responsibility of all educators.

In the final chapter, "Looking Back, Looking Forward," I reflect on the themes and issues explored throughout the text and suggest considerations for, and general approaches to, strengthening the connections between writing and information literacy education, including through continued support and development of compositionist-librarian collaborations. Expanding and deepening these relationships is a long-term project that we might approach with the same openness, curiosity, and persistence that we hope students will bring to their development as writers, researchers, and critical thinkers.

# Chapter 2

## STUDENTS AS WRITERS AND RESEARCHERS: EMPIRICAL STUDIES AND PEDAGOGICAL IMPLICATIONS

Writing is alive when it is being written, read, remembered, contemplated, followed--when it is part of human activity. Otherwise it is dead on the page, devoid of meaning, devoid of influence, worthless. The signs on the page serve to mediate between people, activate their thoughts, direct their attention, coordinate their actions, provide the means of relationship. It is in the context of their activities that people consider texts and give meaning to texts. And it is in the organization of activities that people find the needs, stances, interactions, tasks that orient their attention toward texts they write and read.[1]
- Charles Bazerman and David Russell, *Writing Selves/Writing Societies: Research from Activity Perspectives*

[T]he conceiving of information as a thing—the "reification" of information—has permitted us to treat it as a commodity [...][2] [...] Yet this apparent decontextualization is illusory. Information never stands alone—it is always produced and used in ways that represent social relationships. And these representations and relationships are not merely a matter of chance or individual choice but reflect the underlying patterns that structure society. All information use involves—in Michael Apple's term—"recontextualization," a process by which users make active sense out of the information packets that they encounter.[3]
- Christine Pawley, "Information Literacy: A Contradictory Coupling"

---

1. Charles Bazerman and David R. Russell, eds., *Writing Selves/Writing Societies: Research from Activity Perspectives*, Perspectives on Writing, an Electronic Books Series (Fort Collins, CO: WAC Clearinghouse, 2003), 1.

2. Christine Pawley, "Information Literacy: A Contradictory Coupling," *Library Quarterly* 73, no. 4 (2003): 425.

3. Ibid., 433; Michael W. Apple, *Official Knowledge: Democratic Education in a Conservative Age* (New York: Routledge, 1993), 68.

In 2003, the same year in which the first of Rolf Norgaard's two-part editorial "Writing Information Literacy" appeared, the two texts quoted above were also published.[4] In *Writing Selves/Writing Societies* compositionists Charles Bazerman and David Russell proposed a pedagogy that foregrounds how the social nature of composing gives it meaning and purpose, while library science professor Christine Pawley recommended a similar approach to information literacy instruction, a pedagogy that underscores the social and structural contexts that shape information creation, distribution, and reuse. In emphasizing texts and information as situated within specific communities, conversations, and environments, these scholars articulated social constructivist approaches that had become highly influential in the 1980s and 1990s in composition studies and that were gaining increased attention in librarianship.

Though Bazerman and Russell do not directly refer to information literacy, and Pawley similarly does not call explicit attention to composition studies, the connections between these fields are evident throughout the authors' writings, as are the interrelated pedagogical implications of each text. Just as Bazerman and Russell were questioning teaching that removes the act of writing from social interactions, Pawley was challenging the tendency in libraries and in society more generally to view information and information systems as separate from the larger social relations and conditions that shape them. In other words, Bazerman, Russell, and Pawley all called attention to the inclination (within and beyond the classroom) to overlook the social contexts in which knowledge is created, circumstances that actually give learning its greatest meaning. The social constructivist approaches that their work mirrors have been vital to much of writing pedagogy since the 1960s, when college writing programs began to expand considerably and when composition and rhetoric began to take hold as an academic field. Though the library profession has generally been slower to adopt such pedagogies, most academic librarians today would probably argue

---

4. Rolf Norgaard, "Writing Information Literacy: Contributions to a Concept," *Reference & User Services Quarterly* 43, no. 2 (Winter 2003): 124–30.

that a more rhetorically situated pedagogy that emphasizes the social and communicative functions of information seeking and use is ideal.

While the theses of Bazerman and Russell's and Pawley's above-quoted texts are in many respects remarkably similar, the conversations in which these scholars were engaged appear to have taken place in separate circles. Their work is a reminder of the silos that have existed between the work of compositionists and library professionals. (Reasons for the separation between our professional discourses were touched on in Chapter 1 and are explored more fully in Chapters 4 and 5.) Fortunately that tendency is changing, as is evident in recent conversations about the intersections between the ACRL *Framework for Information Literacy for Higher Education* and the WPA *Framework for Success in Postsecondary Writing*, which are the focal points of Chapter 3.

Bazerman and Russell's argument that the social and communicative functions of writing make it "alive" is likely to be familiar to compositionists and to many librarians. Pawley's argument about the reification of information, however, may be less familiar, perhaps in part because constructivist approaches to library instruction and discussions about the biases of information systems have been slower to develop. As Pawley implies, the term "information" often connotes a sense of objectivity, despite the fact that biased or inaccurate information is still "information," and despite the not uncommon postmodern argument that all knowledge is constructed in some fashion.

Relatedly, the work of librarians and of information literacy instruction has often been perceived, much like library databases and other information retrieval tools, as unbiased and as relatively unaffected by social, cultural, and political contexts. This notion of library neutrality exists in tension with the impossibility of creating library resources and services that are extracted from the social, political, and structural contexts in which they have come to exist. As Pawley argues, librarianship has in many ways constructed and reinforced the perception that libraries and librarians represent a kind of objectivity, and that library resources reflect a purely objective approach to collecting, organizing, and making accessible vast amounts of information. The idea of library neutrality has likely contributed to a lack of dialogue among librarians and compositionists, as it can reinforce the view that library instruction is primarily about mechanical procedures, as well as the perception that librarians engage mainly in perfunctory functions and have little to say about what effective pedagogy and education might look like. Such a perception of library neutrality has increasingly been a point of critique within librarianship, but it continues to play a considerable role in how libraries and library work are perceived in and outside of the profession.[5]

Given the common perception of library work and of library tools as free of any bias, it is perhaps unsurprising that for most college course instructors the phrase "library instruction" calls to mind generic database demonstrations that remain disconnected from the larger context of a course. What is perhaps more surprising is that despite composition studies' emphasis on language and discourse as socially situated, many college writing courses still teach the research process in a fairly linear and mechanical way that may reinforce a decontextualized approach to information seeking and use.[6]

The perception of library resources and services—including library instruction—as existing in a gray space in which information is abstracted from its human context presents an ongoing challenge for instruction librarians who resist a tools-based approach to teaching. While most librarians value instruction that centers on critical thinking, many also understandably struggle with how to implement such a pedagogy given the context in which library instruction most often occurs (that is, a

---

5. For an extensive discussion of the problematic concept of library neutrality see: *Questioning Library Neutrality: Essays from* Progressive Librarian, ed. Alison Lewis (Duluth, MN: Library Juice Press, 2008).

6. James P. Purdy and Joyce R. Walker, "Liminal Spaces and Research Identity: The Construction of Introductory Composition Students as Researchers," *Pedagogy: Critical Approaches to Teaching Literature, Language, Composition, and Culture* 13, no. 1 (Winter 2013): 9–41; Melissa Bowles-Terry, Erin Davis, and Wendy Holliday, "'Writing Information Literacy' Revisited: Application of Theory to Practice in the Classroom," *Reference & User Services Quarterly* 49, no. 3 (2010): 225–30.

single class session for a course taught by another instructor).[7] As noted in Chapter 1, this "one-shot" format, from which many librarians strive to break away, has tended to reinforce the perception of information literacy as an "add-on" that is separate from the writing process and from other instructional goals.

The view of information literacy instruction as an "add-on" may remind many compositionists of a similar struggle for writing instructors. Arno F. Knapper expressed frustration with similar perceptions of writing in his 1978 essay "Good Writing: A Shared Responsibility." "Writing is not a one-shot subject that can be handled in the confines of a single course," he asserted, "but must be stressed over and over again in a student's college career."[8] And yet, Knapper continued,

> Historically, the teachers of writing have borne the burden, responsibility, and blame for teaching or not teaching good writing skills… Alone, the teachers of writing are bound to be less than wholly successful since no one person can possibly possess all the skills and fill all the conditions necessary to achieve a high rate of success in training good writers.[9]

As this reflects, misunderstandings of both writing and information literacy as remedial skills have contributed greatly to the ease with which many educators and administrators over the decades have complained that students can no longer write or think critically. The enduring nature

---

7. Part of this challenge comes not only from a limited amount of time, but also from a desire–and often a sense of obligation among many librarians–to teach all of the content that a course instructor has requested for a class session. In short, there is often a tension between what a librarian would ideally teach and what seems feasible for a given session. Such difficulties are further complicated by the often hierarchical dynamics between librarians and teaching faculty and the structural conditions that influence everyday work in higher education (issues which I explore more fully in Chapter 5).

8. Arno F. Knapper, "Good Writing–a Shared Responsibility," *Journal of Business Communication* 15, no. 2 (Winter 1978): 23.

9. Ibid., 23–24.

of that worry suggests it to be more myth than reality, as Harvey J. Graff has convincingly argued.[10]

The separate efforts of librarians and compositionists to challenge views of writing and information literacy as isolated skills have perhaps detracted our attention from how we might jointly challenge misconceptions of literacy education. That said, there are also rich library-writing partnerships that successfully do this. (Chapter 4 will explore several such examples.) The value of such collaborative work is evident from a sizeable number of empirical studies that demonstrate the benefits of teaching writing and information seeking and use as integrated activities. In this chapter I consider a number of such studies and their pedagogical implications. This research illustrates significant challenges that students face in developing as writers and as researchers. But perhaps more importantly, these studies can inform the development of pedagogies that better support students in engaging in writing and source use as meaningful acts of inquiry and social exchange.

It is worth noting here that when I describe students as researchers in this chapter, I am concentrating on their experiences with source-based research, or in other words, their processes of seeking, selecting, evaluating, and using information. While the act of researching can take many forms that extend beyond this narrow use of the term, this is the kind of research students most often engage in during their undergraduate careers and in writing courses. Such source-based research is often a starting point for students before they engage in other kinds of discipline-specific research.

This chapter's discussion of students' writing, research, and information practices provides a fuller context for considering the growing conversations among compositionists and librarians about pedagogy. It thus serves as a foundation for subsequent chapters, including Chapter 3, which focuses on the WPA *Framework for Success in Postsecondary Writing*

---

10 Harvey J. Graff, "Literacy Crises and Campaigns in Perspective," *Literacy as Social Exchange: Intersections of Class, Gender, and Culture*, 1994, 1; Harvey J. Graff, "The History of Literacy," *Historical Social Research*, no. 34 (April 1985): 37–43.

and the ACRL *Framework for Information Literacy for Higher Education*, and their implications for both our individual and shared teaching. As is considered in Chapter 3, the pedagogical implications of the research studies discussed in this chapter frequently align with the teaching approaches implied in the two frameworks.

The studies explored in this chapter illustrate two major commonalities between writing and information literacy development: 1) the rhetorical and social contexts of writing and information literacy that give them their greatest meaning and 2) the long-term and gradual nature of writing and information literacy development. Taken together, these two themes convey the importance of underscoring the contextual and rhetorical nature of writing and information literacy through long-term and scaffolded instruction. These studies also make evident the important connections between the cognitive and affective domains of learning, which necessarily intersect with students' development as writers, researchers, and participants in various discourse communities. The intersections between the cognitive and affective learning domains that are evident in much of the research described in this chapter are reminders that it is not simply what students can *do* in relation to writing and information use that matters, but also what they think, believe, and experience about themselves as writers and researchers that plays a powerful role in their learning.

These two overarching themes–the rhetorical and social contexts of writing and information literacy and the gradual nature of their development–are considered more specifically in relation to several narrower topics:

- students' identities as writers and researchers;
- students' conceptions of information seeking and use;
- the tendency for information systems and research tools to decontextualize sources; and
- the challenges students often face in recontextualizing such sources.

These studies point to the highly contextual and variable nature of writing and information practices, and thus suggest the importance of pedagogical approaches that promote learning transfer (the ability to apply knowledge and skills developed in one situation to another). The latter part of this chapter, therefore, gives particular attention to this issue of transfer, while drawing on the larger themes of this chapter.

## Social and Affective Dimensions of Writing and Information Literacy Development

As many compositionists have emphasized, writing is a highly social activity when it involves active engagement with a community. Such composing often requires negotiating how one expresses a public and a personal self and is inseparable from students' broader cognitive and social development. It thus makes sense that students' views of themselves as writers and as researchers, and relatedly their conceptions of writing and information use as activities, would play powerful roles in how they approach composing and related information practices.[11] Studies on student writing and information seeking and use indicate again and again that these activities are most meaningful when students see a larger purpose in their work, a social and communicative function that helps them to view themselves as individuals with valuable ideas to share with a community to which they connect. In other words, students' views of themselves as community participants who exchange ideas have a remarkable effect on their long-term development as writers and researchers. Compositionist Paul Rogers highlights this idea when reviewing longitudinal studies of students' writing development. As he observes:

---

11. The affective dimensions of writing and information practices that intersect with these self-conceptions are also key to students' abilities to transfer their learning from one context to another, as is considered further toward the end of this chapter.

while growth in writing abilities is intimately connected to social interactions and is related to other forms of psychological and emotional
change related to identity and self-efficacy, the bulk of detectable
changes exhibited by developing writers are arguably best viewed as
movement toward greater levels of participation in particular communities of practice.[12]

Thus, students are best supported in their development as writers when
presented with meaningful and frequent opportunities to participate
in particular communities of practice, both within and outside of the
traditional classroom.

The long-term studies that Rogers reviews call attention to the fact
that composing abilities develop gradually over time. As Rogers explains
in the opening of his article, "[l]ongitudinal studies [... ] with their
emphasis on change over time and across contexts have proven a particularly appropriate method in understanding writing development."[13]
As Rogers further asserts, the longitudinal research he examined "show[s]
unequivocally that students develop as writers and people throughout
their college experiences through interactions with a variety of sociocultural inputs."[14]

The same argument might be made about for students' development
as researchers and critical information users, and indeed many of the
studies which Rogers discusses frequently examine how students engage
and write with sources. Although longitudinal research on information
literacy development specifically has been far more limited (the Ethnographic Research in Illinois Academic Libraries, or ERIAL, Project
is one exception discussed later in this chapter), the relevance of the
research Rogers outlines to information literacy is evident in these studies'
descriptions of source use and intertextuality. For example, in Elizabeth
Chiseri-Strater's study of two college students' writing development, a

---

12. Paul Rogers, "The Contributions of North American Longitudinal
Studies of Writing in Higher Education to Our Understanding of Writing
Development," in *Traditions of Writing Research*, ed. Charles Bazerman et al.
(New York ; London: Routledge, 2010), 374.

13. Ibid., 365.

14. Ibid., 374.

key part of students' learning was recognizing that "their ideas were never generated totally in isolation" and that "the reading and writing served as a foundation from which writers make new knowledge."[15] As students developed this understanding, their focus shifted from that of a solitary writer to a view of "sources and social contexts from which discourse arises."[16]

Another project which Rogers explores and which has clear relevance to information literacy is Nancy Sommers and Laura Saltz's four-year study of Harvard University students' writing development. In this investigation into how students develop as writers throughout their college education, students frequently engaged in source-based writing and developed their understandings of writing as a means of engaging in larger conversations.[17] This research focused on students as novices who "writ[e] into expertise." Such a long-term view of learning stands in stark contrast to the tradition of one-shot library instruction that has long been the norm in library instruction programs.[18] Sommers and Saltz's research, which looked in large part at source-based writing, has strong relevance to information literacy development and therefore deserves closer attention here.

## Writing as Novices into Expertise

Sommers and Saltz's four-year study of college students' writing is particularly useful for considering the long-term nature of writing and information literacy development and their connections to students' broader cognitive, social, and emotional development. Through study

---

15. Ibid., 369.

16. Elizabeth Chiseri-Strater, *Academic Literacies: The Public and Private Discourse of University Students* (Portsmouth, NH: Boynton/Cook, 1991), 21.

17. Nancy Sommers and Laura Saltz, "The Novice as Expert: Writing the Freshman Year," *College Composition and Communication* 56, no. 1 (2004): 124-49.

18. Longitudinal research on information literacy development has been far more limited than that in composition studies. The Ethnographic Research in Illinois Academic Libraries, or ERIAL, Project is one exception that is discussed later in this chapter.

surveys, interviews, and analysis of writing by students in Harvard University's Class of 2001, the authors explored how students evolve as writers during their college years. Sommers and Saltz give particular attention to how students' attitudes and writing abilities are reflected in the ways they talk about writing and how that language changes over time.[19] The relevance of the study to information literacy is evident in the authors' description of the kinds of writing with which participants engaged, which included assignments that "ask students to work with challenging sources, argue their own ideas, and integrate their arguments into a larger scholarly debate."[20] Sommers and Saltz identify two particularly significant characteristics of student writing development: those students whose writing appeared to develop most significantly during college "initially accept[ed] their status as novices" and "[saw] in writing a larger purpose than fulfilling an assignment."[21] This points to the significance of students' beliefs and attitudes about the purpose of the writing process and their relationship to it.

Sommers and Saltz's work demonstrates the pedagogical value of foregrounding writing and research as social and communicative activities and of inviting students to view themselves as writers and researchers with ideas to contribute to larger conversations. This study has drawn particular attention to what Sommers and Saltz call the "novice-as-expert paradox." Their findings indicate that when students recognize their positions as novices, they are better able to work *toward* the role of expert, in large part because of the dispositions students develop in relation to the composing process. In recognizing themselves as emerging writers, students are more open to new ideas and approaches and thus are better positioned to learn.

> Being a novice [...] involves adopting an open attitude to instruction and feedback, a willingness to experiment [...], and a faith that, with

---

19. Sommers and Saltz, "The Novice as Expert: Writing the Freshman Year," 126.

20. Ibid., 133.

21. Ibid., 124.

practice and guidance, the new expectations of college can be met. Being a novice allows students to be changed by what they learn, to have new ideas, and to understand that 'what the teacher wants' is an essay that reflects these ideas.[22]

In contrast, "those freshmen who cling to their old habits and formulas and who resent the uncertainty and humility of being a novice have a more difficult time adjusting to the demands of college writing."[23] As this implies, affective dimensions of learning like attitudes and dispositions have a significant influence on writing and information literacy development and deserve considerable attention among educators across the disciplines.

Sommers and Saltz's work illustrates the powerful role that students' emerging identities as writers and researchers play in their learning process. As the authors explain, while "it may seem illogical or unfair to ask novices to perform the move of experts," [24] "freshmen build authority not by writing *from* a position of expertise but by writing *into* expertise."[25] This process is, of course, a gradual one. Work like that of Sommers and Saltz suggests that students will benefit from a pedagogy that positions them as developing writers and researchers and that encourages them to explore issues about which they care. This leaves open much room for considering what such a pedagogy might look like. How might an instructor facilitate students' "writing into expertise" while recognizing their novice status in ways that do not dismiss students' voices or experiences? Looking more closely at students' conceptions of research and source use is one productive avenue for exploring this question.

## Conceptions of Information Seeking and Use

Part of the challenge that students face in engaging with sources may be closely tied to their conceptions of sources and of those sources'

---

22. Ibid., 133.
23. Ibid.
24. Ibid.
25. Ibid., 134.

functions in academic writing. A number of studies suggest that students often learn that sources are objects to be inserted into a paper, rather than that they are ideally approached as artifacts that reflect ideas developed and shared in specific social contexts. If students are to approach source-based writing as novices who are open to developing new approaches and understandings, educators across disciplines may need to prompt them to reexamine prior assumptions about source use and source-based writing.

Moreover, teachers might also examine ways that instruction about source-based research sometimes contributes to notions of sources as abstracted citations to be inserted into a paper. A number of studies examining students' and instructors' conceptions of and approaches to source-based research and writing suggest that instruction about the research process often does not encourage inquiry-driven approaches or dispositions toward research such as curiosity. In one such study of how writing students are taught to find and use sources, librarian Wendy Holliday and Intensive English Language professor Jim Rogers perceived a tendency among writing instructors and librarians to emphasize locating sources rather than learning about those sources. Holliday and Rogers observed, moreover, that this has a significant effect on how students approach research and information use. Reflecting on their observations of a college writing course taught by a compositionist and a librarian, interviews with the course instructor, focus groups with students, and analysis of students' course assignments, Holliday and Rogers note that during instruction "[s]ources were often described as **external objects** with attributes that could be identified in order to narrow and complete the research process" (my emphasis).[26] More specifically, instruction about sources frequently underscored finding the "right" number of sources and the "right kind" of sources (meaning peer-reviewed articles, which were contrasted to web sources).[27] Holliday and Rogers contend

---

26. Wendy Holliday and Jim Rogers, "Talking About Information Literacy: The Mediating Role of Discourse in a College Writing Classroom," *portal: Libraries and the Academy* 13, no. 3 (2013): 260.

27. Ibid., 261, 263.

that the way instructors talk about sources and information seeking makes a difference in how students approach information seeking and use. While a discourse focused on finding sources and on "sources as containers" appeared to encourage more surface-level approaches to research, a discourse of "learning about sources" that foregrounded the dialogic nature of creating and exchanging information fostered more inquiry-based, dialectical strategies for engaging with both sources and with research tools used to locate sources. As Holliday and Rogers explain,

> When sources are viewed as containers, it potentially diverts attention away from the content of the sources themselves. Likewise, a discourse of "learning about" directs attention to the content of sources. If internalized, both of these conceptions might serve as psychological tools that mediate how students view and engage in the research process.[28]

This suggests, much like Sommers and Saltz's work, that students' prior experiences and understandings of source use play important roles in how they advance as researchers and as writers. Prior conceptions of source use and of writing may often stand in the way of students' developing new approaches to information and composing practices.

Many students may have previously developed internalized understandings of research and source use, perspectives that have a significant influence on how they engage in research writing. Holliday and Rogers identify a relationship between students' varying conceptions of sources and their information practices:

> From the limited interactions we had with students, it appeared that some of them had already internalized the historically created artifact of source as container. By continuing to limit the discourse on sources, some students also limited their use of the artifact. [...] Other students seemed to take cues from the discourse on "learning about" and embraced a fresh approach to research.[29]

---

28. Ibid., 267.
29. Ibid.

Acknowledging the significant challenge of approaching sources with a more analytical stance, Holliday and Rogers believe that a discourse of "learning about sources" can help students develop more nuanced approaches to sources that indicate a fuller understanding of discourse as dialectical.

Holliday and Rogers' findings are further supported by earlier research in composition and by a number of studies in information science.[30] Among the earliest and most well-known of such work is that of compositionists Robert A. Schwegler and Linda K. Shamoon, who in 1982 explored students' and college instructors' differing conceptions of the purpose and nature of research paper assignments.[31] Through interviews with college students and college instructors from different disciplines, Schwegler and Shamoon found a clear disconnect between students' and professors' perspectives: while teachers viewed research writing as analytical, interpretive, and argumentative, students tended to view such assignments as centered on fact gathering and information reporting. These contrasting views may help to explain college instructors' common frustrations with student writing that resembles a collection of quotes, rather than analysis and argumentation that reflects awareness of one's audience and rhetorical purpose. The teachers in Schwegler and Shamoon's study, however, indicated that they rarely provided explicit guidance to students on how to approach research or source use. (Similarly, library instruction has tended to give limited time to these higher level aspects of information use.)

---

30. Jennie Nelson and John R. Hayes, *How the Writing Context Shapes College Students' Strategies for Writing from Sources*, Technical Report 16 (Berkeley, CA: Center for the Study of Writing,1988); Jennie Nelson, *"This Was an Easy Assignment": Examining How Students Interpret Academic Writing Tasks*, Technical Report 43 (Berkeley, CA: Center for the Study of Writing, 1990); Louise Limberg, "Experiencing Information Seeking and Learning: A Study of the Interaction between Two Phenomena," *Information Research* 5, no. 1 (1999): 50–67; Louise Limberg and Olaf Sundin, "Teaching Information Seeking: Relating Information Literacy Education to Theories of Information Behaviour," *Information Research* 12, no. 1 (2006), http://www.informationr.net/ir/12-1/paper280.html.

31. Robert A. Schwegler and Linda K. Shamoon, "The Aims and Process of the Research Paper," *College English* 44, no. 8 (1982): 817–24.

The discrepancy between instructors' and students' views of source-based writing is likely explained largely by their differing degrees of experience with academic and disciplinary research and writing. Teachers in Schwegler and Shamoon's interviews expressed intuitive understandings of research and disciplinary writing, perspectives that reflected tacit knowledge of disciplinary writing conventions, which these scholars used to evaluate their academic peers' work. Though these discipline-specific conventions were vital to this work, professors did not teach their students about these seemingly intuitive practices. Reflecting on their findings, Schwegler and Shamoon recommend that instructors teach about disciplinary research writing conventions in lower-level undergraduate content courses and in writing courses.

Schwegler and Shamoon's conclusion that there is an important relationship between students' views of and approaches to research writing is further supported by the work of compositionists Jennie Nelson and John R. Hayes. Much of their scholarship in the 1980s and 1990s on students' source-based writing provides evidence that instruction can have a significant impact on how students approach source-based writing. In their 1988 study, the authors examined student writing process logs and writing assignments in order to better understand university students' conceptions of and strategies for source-based writing.[32] Most students approached assignments as a matter of fact-finding, as they used "low-investment" strategies that minimized the amount of research and source analysis involved. However, more advanced students (upper classmen and graduate students) were more likely to apply "high-investment" strategies that reflected an inquiry-based approach of exploring issues.

At the same time that more advanced students in Nelson and Hayes's study were generally more likely to apply more sophisticated research strategies, assignment prompts and instruction also played a significant role in students' approaches to writing with sources: students were far more likely to apply more complex research and writing strategies that

---

32. Nelson and Hayes, "How the Writing Context Shapes College Students' Strategies for Writing from Sources."

entailed fuller analysis, topic development, and strategic searching when assignments were scaffolded and when instructors provided feedback at multiple stages.[33] Sequenced assignments and feedback apparently encouraged students to view writing and source use as more than fact gathering. This suggests that assignment design and related instruction are likely to have significant effects on how students approach research and source use. Viewed together, the work of Holliday and Rogers, Schwegler and Shamoon, and Nelson and Hayes provides compelling evidence that students' conceptions of and attitudes toward inquiry and information seeking and use are significantly influenced by curricula and instruction that occur both during and prior to college.

## Student Research Identities and Pedagogical Practices

Students' conceptions of and approaches to information seeking and use may be better understood when related to their views of themselves as writers and researchers. While the role of "researcher" can take many shapes, I focus here on the kind of research most frequently associated with library instruction: information seeking, source evaluation and selection, and use of sources when communicating one's own ideas.

The importance of students' identities in relation to composing and information practices is apparent in Sommers and Saltz's four-year study on students' development as writers. As discussed earlier in this chapter, Sommers and Saltz found that students who accept their roles as novice writers appear better positioned to develop as writers, likely because they approach their composing processes with greater openness and reflection than do students who believe themselves to have already mastered writing.[34] The role of pedagogy in students' developing identities as researchers is the focal point of one project by compositionists James P. Purdy and Joyce R. Walker. They explored how writing courses approach teaching the research process, giving particular attention to

---

33. Ibid.
34. Sommers and Saltz, "The Novice as Expert."

the relationship between pedagogy and what they call "research identity" (which they define as "the confluence of skills, knowledge, attitudes, and practices that combine when an individual engages in research activities"). The authors relate "research identities" to how students approach not only their academic work, but also their positions as "civic participants."[35]

Though Purdy and Walker's definition of research identity extends beyond simply finding and incorporating sources into one's writing, their discussion of research instruction actually focuses on these particular aspects of the research process.[36] Such teaching, Purdy and Walker suggest, does not always encourage the openness and willingness to experiment that Sommers and Saltz found to be key to developing as a writer. Purdy and Walker analyzed composition handbooks, library websites, and other relevant online resources used in composition courses to teach about the research process, in order to explore how instructional materials encourage or discourage students to develop their research identities. The instructional materials that they examined frequently implied that students should completely abandon their past experiences with online research, since such practices were considered unsuitable for academic purposes. Students' previous research experiences were often presented as irrelevant or even harmful to their academic success, an idea that appears to be based less on fact than on an outmoded conception of "a linear, print-based model of research" that runs counter to the iterative writing process often encouraged in composition studies. As Purdy and Walker assert,

> the new research identities constructed for students through these texts are often based on a linear, print-based model of research, in which a "good" student researcher is one who is efficient and follows only prescribed pathways—pathways that frequently denigrate or deny the experiences of using nonacademic and online research spaces that students bring to academic writing tasks. Being a "good" academic researcher, according to these texts, requires students to leave behind their existing identities as online researchers.[37]

---

35. Purdy and Walker, "Liminal Spaces and Research Identity," 9.

36. Ibid.

37. Ibid.

For example, a chapter in the textbook *Research Strategies for a Digital Age* describes topic development as a task completed before engaging with sources, rather than as an ongoing process that unfolds throughout the research process. As Purdy and Walker point out, such a representation of research resembles earlier cognitive process models of composition which implied that writing is more linear and predictable than it actually is.[38] Purdy and Walker conclude that college writing courses tend to present a formulaic approach to research that does not illustrate the purposes and processes of research and that does not adequately recognize students' identities as researchers.

Such misrepresentations of academic research and of scholarly sources give little attention to the ways in which one's task and purpose can inform one's research approach. These documents thereby present a limited view of research that creates little room for student creativity and exploration. It is important to note that although Purdy and Walker foreground writing curricula in their discussion, a similar argument could be made for library instruction. The tendency in English composition to describe research as linear may, however, seem more surprising, given the extensive work in the field over the past decades that emphasizes writing as a highly recursive process.

Not only might these representations of research prevent students from developing effective approaches to research, they may also discourage students from approaching research with the curiosity, inquisitiveness, and self-motivation that are key to engaged learning. Purdy and Walker thus argue for the importance of acknowledging students' previous research experiences. From Purdy and Walker's perspective, instructional materials about academic research frequently "[p]osition[] students as 'unskilled' or 'illiterate' researchers," and may thereby "damage students' ability to create a 'healthy' academic identity."[39]

One might argue that there is a tension between, on the one hand, Purdy and Walker's argument that students' previous experiences with

---

38. Ibid., 22.
39. Ibid., 26.

information seeking are too readily dismissed, and on the other hand, Sommer and Saltz's stress on the need for students to accept their roles as novices. These two perspectives, however, might work in complementary ways: when students are encouraged to reflect critically on their past experiences and views of information seeking and use, they might consider what has or has not worked and remain open to other approaches. In other words, through metacognitive activities students can draw on prior experiences while also recognizing that their past strategies are not necessarily the most useful for all contexts. Students' acceptance of a novice role in relation to source-based academic research might be particularly important given the apparent tendency among college students of overestimating their information seeking and evaluation skills (as is suggested by numerous research studies).[40]

Purdy and Walker's findings about common approaches to research instruction are further supported by the work of librarians Melissa Terry-Bowles, Erin Davis, and Wendy Holliday, who conducted a similar analysis of composition and library instruction materials several years earlier. They also found that most instructional materials about the research process used in writing classes (and created by both compositionists and librarians) presented research as a linear and procedural process.[41]

Purdy and Walker's views of pedagogy's influence on students' research identities are to a great extent supported by librarians Robert

---

40. Melissa Gross and Don Latham, "Undergraduate Perceptions of Information Literacy: Defining, Attaining, and Self-Assessing Skills," *College & Research Libraries* 70, no. 4 (2009): 336–50; Melissa Gross and Don Latham, "What's Skill Got to Do with It?: Information Literacy Skills and Self-Views of Ability among First-Year College Students," *Journal of the American Society for Information Science and Technology* 63, no. 3 (2012): 574–83, doi:10.1002/asi.21681; M. Gross and D. Latham, "Experiences with and Perceptions of Information: A Phenomenographic Study of First-Year College Students," *Library Quarterly* 81, no. 2 (2011): 161–86, doi:10.1086/658867; Alison J. Head and Michael B. Eisenberg, Truth Be Told: How College Students Evaluate and Use Information in the Digital Age, Project Information Literacy Progress Report (Project Information Literacy, 2010).

41. Bowles-Terry, Davis, and Holliday, "Writing Information Literacy Revisited."

Detmering and Anna Marie Johnson's qualitative study on first-year composition students' emerging identities as researchers. Using student interviews and written "literacy narratives" about students' experiences with locating, evaluating, and using information, Detmering and Johnson found that students' conceptions of sources and of research writing likely have a powerful effect not only on their actual research assignments, but also on their overall dispositions toward (or away from) research. Because college courses often require that students engage with research in unfamiliar ways, their relationships to research are often conflicted and marked by anxiety or even dread. Students involved in this study often described research with negative terms such as "torture," though they also sometimes expressed tentative enthusiasm about a research topic that interested them.

Interestingly, in Detmering and Johnson's study, the students' struggles with their research identities appeared linked to how instructors restricted students' research through, for example, assignment parameters with purposes that were not self-evident.[42] Analysis of these students' narratives suggested that a key factor in students' experiences with academic research is their sense of autonomy and ownership over their research, which often existed in tension with their relationships to their teachers. As Detmering and Johnson explain, students' narratives revealed not only how students conceive of research while negotiating "their often tenuous roles as researchers," but also how students raise larger "questions of authenticity and power in the classroom" (for example, what "counts" as academic research and who has the authority to determine the quality of research).[43]

These narratives also conveyed a common frustration among students about the difficulty of engaging with research writing in a personally meaningful way. Students often described research as menial, or in

---

42. Robert Detmering and Anna Marie Johnson, "'Research Papers Have Always Seemed Very Daunting': Information Literacy Narratives and the Student Research Experience," *portal: Libraries and the Academy* 12, no. 1 (2012): 5–22.

43. Ibid., 6.

the words of one student, as a matter of "spit[ting] out information," "pull[ing] out a bunch of quotes," and "past[ing] together" those quotes in order to create "a collage of plagiarism that people actually accepted as a real paper."[44] In contrast, students conveyed enthusiasm when they felt a personal connection to their topic and thus approached research as a process of inquiry. It appears that students usually expressed uneasy feelings about academic research when they did not feel particularly engaged in their topics.

As these comments imply, and as Detmering and Johnson observe, "[s]tudents want their own voices to be present in the paper. They want the voice to be authentic, but the way that they have conceptualized or understood library or academic research creates a struggle for many of them to achieve what they feel is an authentic piece of 'research.'"[45] Much as in Sommers and Saltz's 2004 study, students' emergence as writers and as researchers appeared closely tied to their developing identities and the expression of their own "voices." In other words, it is when students see a larger social and communicative purpose and meaning in research and writing that they are most engaged in these processes and most motivated to continue developing as researchers and writers.

## Decontextualized Information and the Illusion of Technological Neutrality

Although most college instructors probably want their students to approach source-based writing as an analytical activity, studies that offer a closer look at college teaching practices—like those of Purdy and Walker and of Holliday and Rogers—provide evidence that instructors often present the processes of finding and using sources as primarily mechanical (i.e., use these particular research tools to obtain X number of sources). Though the desired instructional goal might be teaching analytical and rhetorical approaches to source-based research, instruction

---

44. Ibid., 12.
45. Ibid., 13.

often implies that the end goal is gathering objects. This disjunction between pedagogical goals and approaches relates to questions that drive much of this book. Why does instruction about research so often present a formulaic approach that belies how scholars actually do research and how they hope for students to approach research? How can instruction about information seeking and use better support students in developing more purposeful strategies for engaging with sources? I will now give particular attention to how procedural approaches to information literacy instruction may be tied to perceptions of library resources and information retrieval systems (like library databases) as neutral objects.

As noted at the beginning of this chapter, one likely reason for the often mechanical approach taken to teaching the research process is reflected in Pawley's description of information's decontextualization, which is especially evident in library information systems and retrieval tools that cannot provide a very full picture of the context in which sources originate. Pawley, as also quoted in this chapter's opening, writes that "the conceiving of information as a thing—the 'reification' of information—has permitted us to treat it as a commodity [...]."[46] "Yet," she later asserts, "this apparent decontextualization is illusory. Information never stands alone—it is always produced and used in ways that represent social relationships."[47] This decontextualization is especially evident with research tools like Internet search engines and library databases. While such resources serve valuable functions, they also extract information from its original places of creation and distribution, thus making it easy to overlook the context in which that information came to exist and how it relates to other sources and conversations.

The common notion of technology—and more specifically of digital research tools—as neutral may further reinforce a mechanical and linear approach to using search tools. Some studies suggest that the unwarranted degree of trust that students (and probably most individuals) place in search tools to yield unbiased and relevant results may be attributed

46. Pawley, "Information Literacy," 425.

47. Ibid., 433; Apple, *Official Knowledge*, 68.

largely to this illusion of technology as purely objective. Although students frequently report that they have little difficulty finding information online, the very research tools that make information retrieval appear so easy may also mask the importance of carefully evaluating sources. The ease of retrieving some kind of information—even if that material is not the most relevant—may help to explain students' tendencies to overestimate their information seeking abilities.

As anthropologist and librarian Andrew Asher explains, although no search system can be entirely neutral, students (and most Internet users) have learned to place significant trust in search engines and their relevance rankings to provide accurate and unbiased search results.[48] Such an overreliance on the "accuracy" of Internet search engines appears to have greatly influenced students' approaches to library database searching as well. As has been illustrated by a number of empirical studies, students tend to choose the first few information sources retrieved through their information searches.[49] When asked about their search strategies, these students frequently describe this strategy as effective.[50] (This tendency is not unique to students, as is suggested by other research on information seeking behaviors).[51]

---

48. Andrew Asher, "Search Epistemology: Teaching Students about Information Discovery," in *Not Just Where to Click: Teaching Students How to Think about Information*, ed. Troy A. Swanson and Heather Jagman, Publications in Librarianship 68 (Chicago, IL: Association of College and Research Libraries, 2015), 139–54.

49. Ibid.; Head and Eisenberg, *Truth Be Told*; Ruth Mirtz, "Encountering Library Databases: Nextgen Students' Strategies for Reconciling Personal Topics and Academic Scholarship," in *The New Digital Scholar: Exploring and Enriching the Research and Writing Practices of NextGen Students*, ed. Randall McClure and James P. Purdy, ASIS&T Monograph Series (American Society for Information Science and Technology, 2013), 189–207; Dave Green, "The ERIAL Project: Findings, Ideas, and Tools to Advance Your Library," Conference Paper Summary, Association of College and Research Libraries, 2013, http://www.ala.org/acrl/sites/ala.org.acrl/files/content/conferences/confsandpreconfs/2013/papers/Green_summary.pdf.

50. Asher, "Search Epistemology: Teaching Students about Information Discovery."

51. Bernard J. Jansen and Amanda Spink, "How Are We Searching the World Wide Web? A Comparison of Nine Search Engine Transaction Logs," *Information Processing & Management* 42, no. 1 (2006): 248–63; Michaël R. Laurent

Add to this the common practice among teachers, including librarians, to instruct students that databases are superior to Google because they include more "authoritative" sources. This reinforces the view that research tools will yield relevant and useful results; it also suggests that the search tool through which one locates information is an accurate, or at least sufficient, proxy for determining a source's credibility.

Such trust in search engine and database relevance rankings is apparent in students' uses of library discovery tools ("super" databases that search across library databases and catalogs in order to provide a more seamless search experience that more closely resembles that of Google searching). In a study of eighty-seven undergraduate students' work with discovery tools, Asher observed individual students as they searched for sources for a hypothetical research assignment. Asher also conducted semi-structured interviews with students about their research and information searching experiences while working on the research assignment. These students rarely evaluated sources with much depth, rarely looked past the first page of search results, and almost never used more search strategies beyond keyword searching. As Asher observes, "[b]ecause of this belief that the most credible [...] sources should be found on the first page of search results, students often assumed that if they could not quickly locate information then it must not exist."[52] The study findings suggest that

> While discovery tools (as well as nonlibrary search tools like Google and Google Scholar) have probably reduced the 'cognitive load' exacted by libraries' various and fragmented [...] [research tools], the practices supported by these tools can reinforce unreflective search habits that diminish the overall quality of the information found and used and, by extension, the synthesis of an academic argument.[53]

---

and Tim J. Vickers, "Seeking Health Information Online: Does Wikipedia Matter?" *Journal of the American Medical Informatics Association* 16, no. 4 (2009): 471–79.

52. Asher, "Search Epistemology: Teaching Students about Information Discovery," 145.

53. Ibid., 144.

The purpose of locating sources may get lost amidst information overload and a focus on fulfilling basic assignment requirements.

It is worth reiterating that students are probably not the only individuals who place too much reliance on the relevance rankings of information retrieval systems. Our culture as a whole has become accustomed to turning to search engines like Google for information that quickly answers our questions. These digital tools have become so central to our everyday lives that they are often taken at face value, as if they are immune to reflecting bias. This illusion of neutrality may be exacerbated when using resources like library databases, since such tools are often presented and viewed as offering higher-quality and more authoritative information. Asher notes that individuals, including academics, often mistakenly approach library databases as neutral tools. A deeper understanding of how search tools organize and retrieve information may help students to recognize them as imperfect systems and to develop more sophisticated search strategies, while also approaching source evaluation and selection with deeper thought. Asher recommends that librarians (and, I would add, other educators) teach students about how search systems and relevance rankings generally work, while also placing a greater emphasis on closer evaluation of sources themselves.[54] Asher's recommendations are a reminder that, while many college classes emphasize critical thought in relation to specific subject matter, the constructed nature of search tools is usually overlooked in our everyday lives and in the classroom. Instead, information literacy instruction can stress a critical approach to both individual sources and to the search tools through which they are located.

Librarian and writing instructor Ruth Mirtz describes the decontextualized nature of the sources located through databases and search engines as a "disembodiment" of information sources. Because search results are removed from the contexts in which the represented sources have been created and circulated, it is easy to forget the rhetorical contexts in which those materials came to be. Those sources may appear removed therefore from the "real" world. Thus, it is also easy for the

---

54. Ibid., 147.

research process itself to become perfunctory and for researchers to become disconnected from their research purpose. Mirtz's description of "disembodied sources" closely aligns with Pawley's idea of decontextualized information.

The common assumption that library databases are relatively free of bias, Mirtz argues, may help to explain why English composition scholars have tended to focus on the writing of the research paper, while giving limited attention to how searching for sources affects the writing process.[55] In 2008 (about five years before Asher's Discovery Tools Project), Mirtz sought to address this gap in the writing studies literature by conducting a study of the database search processes used by eighteen first-year college students who were locating sources for a research assignment. Many of her findings closely resemble those of the Discovery Tools Project: students rarely looked past the first page of databases' search results, seldom tried using alternate terms after initially unsuccessful searches, and were more likely to change their research topic according to what was most convenient to find, rather than trying alternative strategies. If students did not find relevant sources immediately, they seemed to believe relevant sources did not exist. As Mirtz explains,

> The way students [...] used library databases indicates that they saw themselves as subjects with a linear, single purpose, independent of variables. The students [...] apparently learned that database searching is like rummaging around in a stranger's attic full of random items saved over the years.[56]

The idea that locating useful sources depends largely on luck rather than on strategic searching suggests not only a limited understanding of how databases are organized and used effectively, but also the difficulty of conceiving of sources as intertextual and representative of larger

---

55. Mirtz, "Encountering Library Databases: Nextgen Students' Strategies for Reconciling Personal Topics and Academic Scholarship," 193.

56. Ibid., 201.

conversations within a given community. As Mirtz notes, "[s]tudents' sense of authority, thus, becomes as disembodied as the articles in the databases."[57] Students struggle to recognize the larger context in which these sources have come into existence and in which they have been organized. Moreover, students likely experience themselves as removed from their research topics, rather than as having something valuable to say about those topics.

To address the sense of "disembodied" research that often occurs during information searches, Mirtz asserts the need for illustrating "how the databases are a kind of conversation among the scholarly community and are only apparently random, as one's Twitter feeds might look to a stranger." Drawing on the work of Mark Poster, she argues for approaching database searching as, like the writing process, part of the rhetorical situation one considers when engaging with a research assignment.[58] Such an approach reflects connections between writing studies and information literacy that have received limited attention, but which are central to helping students engage with all aspects of research as rhetorically situated activities.

Similar recommendations have been made in light of high school students' approaches to evaluating sources online. Information science professor Andrea Forte describes students' different approaches to source evaluation in terms of "first-order" strategies (i.e. heuristics) and "second-order" strategies that require more critical thinking. Students in her study tended to use surface-level approaches to searching and to selecting sources when choosing from a list of sources ranked by relevance in a search engine like Google.[59] However, when creating writing content in online participatory environments like Wikipedia, students

---

57. Ibid.

58. Ibid.; Mark Poster, "Databases as Discourse; or, Electronic Interpellations," in *Computers, Surveillance, and Privacy*, ed. David Lyon and Elia Zureik (Minneapolis: University of Minnesota Press, 1996), 175–92.

59. Andrea Forte, "The New Information Literate: Open Collaboration and Information Production in Schools," *International Journal of Computer-Supported Collaborative Learning* 10, no. 1 (2015): 41, doi:10.1007/s11412-015-9210-6.

often used second-order strategies for source evaluation, demonstrating awareness of how information is produced and the particular purposes of their tasks.[60]

Forte, remarking on the sense of ownership in creating and sharing knowledge that students expressed when creating content in public information sources like Wikipedia, concludes that students' abilities to engage in second-order evaluation strategies are due largely to their experiences in belonging to a community of collaborative peers and writing to a real, public audience.[61] To extend Mirtz's metaphor of dis-embodiment, research appears then to be embodied, connected to life and to students' experiences. Forte's conclusions appear in keeping with Mirtz's argument that in order for students to evaluate and to use sources in more nuanced ways, they need to understand the social contexts in which those sources came to exist, rather than seeing them merely as objects retrieved through a supposedly neutral algorithm. Similarly, Asher believes that teaching students about how search tools function can help them to recognize research tools as socially constructed objects whose results may not always yield the most relevant information.

## Recontextualizing within Unfamiliar Conversations and Environments

Evaluating and using sources in the more sophisticated ways that Mirtz, Asher, and Forte describe, of course, is by no means easy. This is evident in research like that of the Citation Project. A multi-institutional research initiative, the Citation Project's larger aim is to address concerns about student plagiarism by examining how students use sources in their college writing assignments. The project's key findings have raised serious concerns about students' abilities to critically read, comprehend, and use sources and have encouraged college educators to reconsider how students are taught about source use.

---

60. Ibid., 35.
61. Ibid., 48.

The Citation Project's pilot study, "Writing from Sources, Writing from Sentences," illuminates the difficulty for students of analyzing and integrating sources into their own writing. This research offers a fuller context for understanding student plagiarism and the challenges of working with academic sources. In a study of eighteen college student research texts, compositionists Rebecca Moore Howard, Tricia Serviss, Tanya K. Rodrigue found that none of them included a summary of a source.[62] Instead, students "paraphrased, copied from, or 'patchwrote' from individual sentences in their sources," practices that suggest limited understanding and analysis of the sources used.[63] This tendency appears to extend beyond the study's more limited sample size. In a subsequent multi-institutional study of student papers from sixteen U.S. colleges and universities, Jamieson and Howard found similar results: ninety-four percent of students' citations were created at the sentence level, rather than summarizing main ideas from a larger text. Most students also appeared to have read only the first few pages of texts, as forty-six percent of citations came from page one of a given source, sixty-nine percent from the first two pages, and eighty-three percent from the first four pages.[64] The authors conclude that students' heavy use of direct quotes and of patchwriting is less likely a sign of laziness than an indication of a stage in their writing development. Given the significant challenge of comprehending academic texts, students will

---

62. Rebecca Moore Howard, Tricia Serviss, and Tanya K. Rodrigue, "Writing from Sources, Writing from Sentences," *Writing and Pedagogy* 2, no. 2 (2010): 177–92.

63. Ibid., 177. Howard has defined patchwriting as "[c]opying from a source text and then deleting some words, altering grammatical structures, or plugging in one-for-one synonym-substitutions" (Rebecca Moore Howard, "A Plagiarism Pentimento," *Journal of Teaching Writing* 11, no. 3 [1992]: 233).

64. Sandra Jamieson and Rebecca Moore Howard, "Sentence-Mining: Uncovering the Amount of Reading and Reading Comprehension in College Writers' Researched Writing," in *The New Digital Scholar: Exploring and Enriching the Research and Writing Practices of NextGen Students*, ed. Randall McClure and James P. Purdy, ASIS&T Monograph Series (American Society for Information Science and Technology, 2013), 125.

likely need extensive practice in reading and interpreting such sources before they can be expected to write about them in more nuanced ways.

Reflecting on these and other Citation Project studies, Jamieson and Howard argue that these findings point to "a compelling need to overhaul the teaching of researched writing in college classes."[65] The pedagogy they propose would require that students "talk *with* and *about* a source rather than merely mine sentences from it." This, they explain, "involves walking students through texts and modeling for them the kind of engaged reading and rereading that we expect of them."[66] Holliday and Rogers echo this idea in their later study on the discourses used to describe information seeking and use. As noted earlier, they recommend using a discourse of "learning about sources" over a discourse of "sources as containers."[67] Such approaches to teaching can be a joint effort among educators. As Jamieson and Howard assert: "We hope that our campus librarians and our faculty colleagues in writing programs across the disciplines will take these findings as a mandate for instructional change."[68]

While the Citation Project has concentrated on how students' source use is demonstrated in writing assignments, other studies have given more attention to how students navigate libraries and research tools (like library databases and Google) while completing research assignments and other coursework. Project Information Literacy (PIL) is perhaps the most well-known and expansive research project concerning how students seek and use information in university settings. Since 2008, PIL has been conducting large-scale national studies of young adults and their information behaviors. This research demonstrates a need for college instruction and curricula to address more fully the challenges of information seeking and use, particularly in the digital age.

---

65. Ibid., 130.

66. Ibid.

67. Holliday and Rogers, "Talking About Information Literacy."

68. Jamieson and Howard, "Sentence-Mining: Uncovering the Amount of Reading and Reading Comprehension in College Writers' Researched Writing," 130.

Although discussions about how students search for information and how they use sources in their writing often appear somewhat disconnected, the 2009 PIL study *Finding Context: What Today's College Students Say about Conducting Research in the Digital Age* illustrates that key principles of writing—like the context-dependent nature of composing—are also essential to information searching.[69] Drawing on findings from eleven focus groups conducted with students at seven U.S. colleges and universities, the PIL authors Alison J. Head and Michael B. Eisenberg conclude that among the greatest challenges for students in conducting research in the digital age is determining the context for which they will use information. As the authors report:

> Context, as we came to understand it in the sessions, is a key to understanding how students operationalize and prioritize their course-related and everyday life research activities. In our discussions, students consistently referred to "finding context," in one form or another, as the most laborious, yet requisite, part of the research process.[70]

The authors identify four context types that students sought during their research:

- big picture (which involves selecting and defining a topic and recognizing different sides of an argument);
- language (such as terms and discourse related to a topic);
- situational (determining parameters of a topic and expectations for the task); and
- information gathering (finding and accessing relevant resources).[71]

---

69. Alison J. Head and Michael B. Eisenberg, *Finding Context: What Today's College Students Say about Conducting Research in the Digital Age*. Project Information Literacy Progress Report. University of Washington's Information School, February 4, 2009, http://projectinfolit.org/images/pdfs/pil_progressreport_2_2009.pdf.

70. Ibid., 5.

71. Ibid., 5–9.

Both "everyday life" research and course-related research presented significant difficulties for students, though they reported that the latter was far more confusing. The challenges students described included "[n]ot knowing what to look for, yet still sifting through articles that might fit," "[f]eeling that nothing new is being said" and that one is simply seeing "the same information again and again," and "[i]nformation overload."[72]

The finding that students seek to contextualize their research process from various angles is encouraging, given the importance of that process for meaningful inquiry. The effort that students gave to determining a context for their research also supports the Citation Project's conclusions that student plagiarism is likely due less to a lack of effort on students' part than to the challenge of this process of contextualization. As Head and Eisenberg reflect, "[i]n general, students reported being challenged, confused, and frustrated by the research process, despite the convenience, relative ease, or ubiquity of the Internet." Common frustrations included information overload and the continually-changing and vast nature of digital information environments, which tend to extract information from its origins.[73] PIL participants' considerable struggle with and inexperience in determining context during their research suggests the importance of expanding instruction on the purpose of research in specific contexts.

The idea that students do not receive sufficient instruction in college about determining the contexts that should inform their research process is further supported by another PIL study conducted in 2010. In this case, the researchers analyzed 191 course-related research assignment handouts given to undergraduates at twenty-eight colleges in the U.S.[74] Most handouts emphasized procedural standards like the inclusion of a bibliography and the number of sources to use, while most assignments did not include information about more challenging aspects of research, like narrowing a topic or developing a research question. The stress that

---

72. Ibid., 4.

73. Ibid., 13.

74. Head and Eisenberg, *Truth Be Told.*

most assignment handouts place on basic assignment requirements likely contributes to giving less attention to using sources in purposeful ways. And while it is likely that students received further guidance about their assignments that was not included in these handouts, many of these materials often included guidance that does not accurately reflect how information is accessed through library collections today. For example, sixty percent of assignments emphasized consulting library shelves more than library databases, catalogs, or other online resources, despite the fact that most libraries' digital collections are now much more extensive than their print materials. Moreover, few handouts recommended speaking with a librarian (a reminder that the partnerships between academic librarians and course instructors at most institutions is not as strong as we might like).[75] This study, Head and Eisenberg conclude, "suggest[s] that handouts for academic research assignments provide students with more how-to procedures and conventions for preparing a final product for submission, than guidance about conducting research and finding and using information in the digital age."[76] This becomes more concerning when related to the 2009 PIL study "Finding Context,"[77] which indicates a clear need for greater guidance for students in determining their research purpose and seeking information in digital information environments.

PIL's conclusions are supported by similar findings of the ERIAL Project (Ethnographic Research in Illinois Academic Libraries). The ERIAL Project, like Project Information Literacy, explored how students use information and libraries in university settings, as it focused on what students do when given a research assignment. In this two-year study, conducted at five Illinois colleges and universities from 2008 to 2010, anthropologists and librarians employed a range of qualitative research methods, including interviews, photo journals, mapping diaries,

---

75. Ibid., 40.

76. Ibid., 1.

77. Head and Eisenberg, *Finding Context: What Today's College Student Say about Conducting Research in the Digital Age.*

and research journals, in order to gain a fuller picture of how students do academic research, what challenges they encounter, and how they seek help.[78]

While the researchers initially expected that students would have difficulty with using library search tools like databases, they found that once students had basic training on these resources, technology was not the greatest obstacle. Rather, the most challenging aspects of research for students related to activities like reading and understanding citations, comprehending cataloging and information organization systems, developing search strategies beyond simplistic "Google-style" searching, and locating and evaluating resources of all types.[79] As one of the researchers commented, students at all five institutions "seemed lost at almost every step in searching, retrieving, and comprehending the nature of the information they had found, whether online or in print."[80]

This again indicates a need for information literacy instruction that stresses larger rhetorical contexts and purposes that drive inquiry. Moreover, it suggests the pedagogical value of emphasizing conceptual understandings over mechanical procedures, since students' conceptions of sources and source use appear to significantly influence how they approach writing and source use. As I will discuss next, a pedagogical focus on rhetorical context and conceptual understandings is likely to help students not only in finding relevance in a specific writing or research task, but also in engaging in writing and information practices across a range of disciplines and contexts.

---

78. ERIAL Project, "Ethnographic Research in Illinois Academic Libraries: Methodology," 2016, www.erialproject.org/project-details/methodology/.

79. Andrew Asher, Lynda Duke, and David Green, "The ERIAL Project: Ethnographic Research in Illinois Academic Libraries," *The Academic Commons*, May 17, 2010, http://www.academiccommons.org/2014/09/09/the-erial-project-ethnographic-research-in-illinois-academic-libraries/.

80. Green, "The ERIAL Project: Findings, Ideas, and Tools to Advance Your Library (Paper Summary)."

## Learning Transfer: Writing and Researching across Contexts

Learning transfer, the ability for individuals to apply concepts, knowledge, and skills used in one situation to another, has been of significant interest to compositionists for some time. More recently, it has become a wider topic of conversation among instruction librarians. Transfer's importance to writing and library instruction is perhaps most evident in the fact that, although writing and information practices can vary greatly from one context to another, composition and library instruction usually are intended to help students develop skills that can be applied in various situations. In composition studies the "transfer question" (whether transfer happens and if so under what conditions) has been a significant point of debate and research in recent decades. Undergraduate writing courses are usually intended to support students in developing generalized abilities that will enable them to succeed through their education, but most writing occurs in very specific contexts, each of which has its own unique composing conventions and criteria for good writing. Whether or not students are able to transfer their learning across situations thus has significant implications for first-year writing programs.

The same can be said for library instruction, which is also usually intended to teach transferable skills. As library instruction becomes more informed by pedagogical research and theories, librarians' interests in transfer research are growing, though scholarship in this area is still quite limited. As Rebecca Z. Kuglitsch argues, librarians might look to work in composition studies in order to develop instructional models that foster learning transfer for information literacy.[81] An increasing amount of research on transfer supports the idea that transfer is far more likely to occur when an instructor teaches for it.

As compositionists Nancy Blake Yancey, Liane Robertson, and Kara Taczak explain in *Writing Across Contexts: Transfer, Composition, and Sites*

---

81. Rebecca Z. Kuglitsch, "Teaching for Transfer: Reconciling the Framework with Disciplinary Information Literacy," *portal: Libraries and the Academy* 15, no. 3 (2015): 466.

*of Writing,* early research on transfer (most of which was conducted in the fields of education and psychology) suggested that transfer occurs mainly by serendipity and thus cannot be taught. However, the earlier research on transfer occurred in highly controlled conditions that did not resemble real-life situations in which transfer might normally occur. Views about teaching transfer began to shift significantly around 1992, when David Perkins and Gavriel Salomon recommended examining the conditions and contexts in which transfer might occur. Perkins and Salomon argued that transfer is possible when an instructor teaches for it and gives attention to the conditions and contexts in which that learning and transfer are intended to occur.[82] Since the time of Perkins and Salomon's early work, a growing amount of research supports the idea that teaching for transfer is possible.

Perhaps the most comprehensive publication on research in learning transfer is the National Council of Research's 2000 publication, *How People Learn. How People Learn* discusses education research from the past four decades in order to offer a fuller picture of human learning. Though the book's recommendations for teaching are described in relation to teaching and teacher preparation more generally, they are especially relevant to teaching for transfer. The authors identify three key implications for teaching that are informed by their extensive research:

1. "Teachers must draw out and work with the preexisting under-standings that their students bring with them."[83]
2. "Teachers must teach some subject matter in depth, providing many examples in which the same concept is at work and pro-viding a firm foundation of factual knowledge."[84]

---

82. Kathleen Blake Yancey, Liane Robertson, and Kara Taczak, *Writing Across Contexts: Transfer, Composition, and Sites of Writing* (Logan: Utah State University Press, 2014), 6–7; David N. Perkins and Gavriel Salomon, "Transfer of Learning," *Educational Leadership* 46, no. 1 (1988): 22–32.

83. National Research Council (U.S.) et al., *How People Learn: Brain, Mind, Experience, and School,* Expanded edition (Washington, D.C: National Academies Press, 2000), 19.

84. Ibid., 20.

3. "The teaching of metacognitive skills should be integrated into the curriculum in a variety of subject areas."[85]

These points resonate with much of the work in writing and rhetoric on students' writing development. For example, Sommers and Saltz's four-year study of college students' writing development (discussed earlier in this chapter's section "Writing as Novices into Expertise") gives considerable attention to the first point: that teachers encourage students to examine and work with their preexisting understandings. Related to this is the fact that prior learning, when based on incorrect information or assumptions, can prevent new learning. This is often called negative transfer. (Again, Sommers and Saltz found that students who accepted their roles as novices experienced the greatest gains in developing their writing, while students who were initially more skilled writers but who held onto old views of composing progressed far less and were ultimately less sophisticated writers.) Sommers and Saltz's research suggests that students' prior conceptions of writing, if unacknowledged, can stand in the way of advancing their abilities. On the other hand, when students accept their roles as novices they may be more open to new understandings of and approaches to writing.[86]

These findings align with Giyoo Hatano and Kayoko Inagaki's idea of "adaptive expertise."[87] As explained in *How People Learn*, when individuals "realize that what they know is miniscule compared to all that is potentially knowable," they are more likely to transfer learning across situations because they "are able to approach new situations flexibly and to learn throughout their lifetimes."[88] Through adaptive expertise

---

85. Ibid., 21.

86. Sommers and Laura Saltz, "The Novice as Expert."

87. Giyoo Hatano and Kayoko Inagaki, "Two Courses of Expertise," in *Child Development and Education in Japan*, ed. H. W. Stevenson, H. Azuma, and K. Hakuta, A Series of Books in Psychology (New York: W.H. Freeman/Times Books/ Henry Holt & Co., 1986), 262–72.

88. National Research Council (U.S.) et al., *How People Learn*, 48; Nancy J. Vye et al., "Complex Mathematical Problem Solving by Individuals and Dyads," *Cognition and Instruction* 15, no. 4 (1997): 435–84.

an individual develops creative, flexible approaches to a task or problem when unique or new situations are encountered. Because the context is different, an approach that might work well in another situation must be adapted.[89]

This suggests that the attitudes and dispositions one brings to learning play an important role in the potential for learning transfer. According to *How People Learn*, these dispositions and attitudes can be drawn out, explored, or developed through metacognitive activities. (As noted previously, *How People Learn*'s third main conclusion is the value of curricula that foster metacognition.) The importance of dispositions and attitudes to learning transfer is further reflected in composition research on students' motivations for their writing. For example, Linda Bergmann and Janet Zepernick found that when first-year writing students did not perceive that their course writing had relevance to their other studies, they experienced a lack of motivation. These students' writing in later courses suggested little evidence of learning transfer.[90] In contrast, when students are told that transfer is an intended goal of their courses, they may be more motivated to develop their composing abilities, as Tracy Ann Robinson and Vicki Tolar Burton found.[91]

Giving time to students' preexisting knowledge and dispositions may mean slowing the pace at which new content is presented. This is in line

---

89. Hatano and Inagaki, "Two Courses of Expertise."

90. Interestingly, students in Bergmann and Zepernick's study ascribed the composition course's perceived irrelevance to the personal and subjective nature of the writing associated with these classes. Perhaps because this writing was so different from what was expected of students in other courses, they had difficulty relating the work done in the composition classes to what they viewed as "the objective, fact-based, information-telling writing demanded elsewhere in their academic and professional lives"(Linda S. Bergmann and Janet Zepernick, "Disciplinarity and Transfer: Students' Perceptions of Learning to Write," *WPA: Writing Program Administration* 31, no. 1–2 [2007]: 131).

91. Tracy Ann Robinson and Vicki Tolar Burton, "The Writer's Personal Profile: Student Self Assessment and Goal Setting at Start of Term," *Across the Disciplines: Interdisciplinary Perspectives on Language, Learning, and Academic Writing* 6, Special Issue: WAC and Assessment (December 3, 2009), http://wac.colostate.edu/atd/assessment/robinson_burton.cfm.

with *How People Learn*'s second main takeaway for teaching: that depth of subject content is more important than breadth, and that this content should be related to core concepts that help students see their learning in relation to a larger picture. Such a pedagogical approach is supported by the research described in *How People Learn* on how experts organize knowledge and approach problems by working from a conceptual framework. The authors identify several features of expert knowledge that differ from that of novices, including noticing "meaningful patterns of information" and organizing an extensive amount of knowledge "in ways that reflect a deep understanding of their subject matter."[92] These characteristics of expertise suggest that instruction ideally should encourage students to develop their own conceptual understandings of the subject matter about which they are learning. As stated in *How People Learn*, "[t]he fact that experts' knowledge is organized around important ideas or concepts suggests that curricula should also be organized in ways that lead to conceptual understanding." However, this is often difficult to do because of an emphasis in much of curriculum design on covering an extensive amount of content. As the authors assert, "[o]ften there is only superficial coverage of facts before moving on to the next topic; there is little time to develop important, organizing ideas."[93] Reducing the amount of instructional content allows more time for engaging with concepts and conceptual frameworks and may thus be a far more effective way of supporting learning.

The process-oriented nature of writing and information practices might initially appear to be at odds with a pedagogy centered on developing conceptual frameworks, since writing and information literacy are often viewed as skills taught in the service of other academic disciplines, rather than as areas of study in their own right. But the extensive scholarship on writing and information literacy makes clear that writing and information practices are indeed complex areas of study that are informed by broader concepts and conceptual frameworks. Compositionists Douglas Downs and Elizabeth Wardle, frustrated by the difficulty

---

92. National Research Council (U.S.) et al., *How People Learn*, 31.

93. Ibid., 42.

of teaching general writing courses that are not situated within a disciplinary context, argue that using writing studies as the disciplinary lens for introductory writing courses will help students develop strong writing abilities that can be applied across contexts. They propose a "Writing about Writing" (WAW) model for composition courses. This WAW model is founded on the idea that when writing courses teach about composition as a discipline in its own right, rather than as something done only in the service of other disciplines, students are more likely to develop transferable skills and a deeper understanding of the writing process. Downs and Wardle's WAW curriculum provides further evidence that such teaching approaches can be effective. In their first-year WAW courses, they found that students conveyed greater self-awareness of their writing skills, developed fuller understandings of research writing as conversational, and improved their reading abilities and confidence.[94]

A similar approach to information literacy instruction, one that approaches information literacy as an area of study and that encourages students to develop their own conceptual frameworks about information creation, distribution, circulation, and use, appears to guide the thinking behind the ACRL *Framework for Information Literacy for Higher Education*, which is structured by six intersecting conceptual understandings considered essential to information literacy. Though this document does not explicitly mention transfer, transfer's relevance is evident throughout the text in descriptions of information literacy as "extending the arc of learning throughout students' academic careers" and as a shared responsibility of librarians, faculty, and students.[95] This suggests that the ACRL *Framework*, put in conversation with work on learning transfer, can be a valuable tool for teaching about information through a more conceptual lens.

Yancey, Robertson, and Taczak have drawn on Downs and Wardle's WAW model, as well as other research on transfer, in developing a

94. Douglas Downs and Elizabeth Wardle, "Teaching about Writing, Righting Misconceptions: (Re)envisioning 'First-Year Composition' as 'Introduction to Writing Studies,'" *College Composition and Communication* 58, no. 4 (2007): 572–573.

95. Association of College and Research Libraries, *Framework*.

"Teaching for Transfer" (TFT) writing curriculum. This curriculum is also heavily informed by the research gathered in *How People Learn*. In their book *Writing Across Contexts*, Yancey, Robertson, and Taczak discuss how such work on transfer has informed their TFT curriculum, which was the focus of their own study on writing transfer.[96] The authors draw particular attention to *How People Learn*'s discussion of novices' and experts' differing behaviors and what this suggests about teaching that foregrounds metacognitive thinking and conceptual frameworks. The TFT course sought to promote transfer through three interrelated approaches:

1. The introduction of key concepts and terms that provided a language through which to think about writing conceptually
2. Reflective writing activities in which students considered their experiences with course writing assignments
3. A cumulative writing assignment in which students drew on key vocabulary and earlier reflective writing in order to articulate their own theory of writing [97]

To evaluate whether the TFT curriculum proved effective, Yancey, Robertson, and Taczak conducted student and instructor interviews, analyzed student writing samples, and analyzed course materials in the TFT course and in two other sections of first-year composition. They found that students who had enrolled in the TFT course were more likely in future semesters to have transferred the developed writing knowledge and abilities because they "had the advantage of a language and framework they had made their own."[98] The key concepts and terms introduced in the TFT course offered a vocabulary through which students could "create[] a composing passport to help them cross new

---

96. Yancey, Robertson, and Taczak, *Writing across Contexts*.
97. Ibid., 67.
98. Ibid., 65.

writing boundaries."[99] These findings support the researchers' hypothesis that students would gain a deeper understanding of writing through a course that was "organized through key terms or concepts rather than through a set of assignments or processes."[100]

Though some library instruction also emphasizes conceptual understandings and metacognition, and though these are also key elements of the ACRL *Framework*, at the time of this writing I am not aware of similar "teaching for transfer" curricula that have been applied to information literacy instruction. Such a pedagogy could likely be relevant to a growing number of credit-bearing information literacy courses. (I am currently exploring the possibilities for such a curriculum for an undergraduate information literacy course that I teach.) The growing amount of scholarship on teaching information literacy through the lens of conceptual understandings suggests that related scholarship can richly inform such approaches to teaching for transfer.

Librarians and compositionists might also explore together ways that teaching information literacy and writing as integrated processes can promote transfer. (Yancey, Robertson, and Taczak's curriculum does indeed reflect connections between information literacy and writing, though their focus is understandably foremost on writing as an area of study.) Given the complexity of developing conceptual frameworks about writing and information literacy, I would conjecture that in many cases (especially in introductory courses) a "teaching for transfer" curriculum will likely be more effective if it focuses primarily on either writing or information literacy as an area of study. In either of these scenarios, however, intersections between writing and information literacy will likely help in conveying the larger social and communicative functions of writing and information practices. A "teaching for transfer" curriculum that centers heavily on the intersections between writing and information studies might be more effective in specialized, upper-level

---

99. Ibid., 76.
100. Ibid., 40.

courses in which students have already gained some exposure to and practice with academic writing and research.

Composition research on transfer often addresses many conceptual dimensions of information practices, though to my knowledge there has not been research focused on learning transfer when writing and information literacy are approached through a shared conceptual lens. The recent attention given to the role of conceptual understandings and frameworks to both writing and information literacy education presents opportunities for exploring this question further through empirical research and through everyday teaching practices. Recent collaborations between compositionists and librarians interested in the ACRL *Framework for Information Literacy for Higher Education* and the WPA *Framework for Success in Postsecondary Writing* suggest such possibilities. Chapter 4 discusses several such collaborations more fully.

The research studies and pedagogical approaches explored throughout this chapter have implications for transfer. They suggest that as librarians and writing instructors hope for students to apply their learning to situations outside of our classrooms, students need to be given more opportunities to reflect on their writing and information practices in various contexts, as well as to draw connections between those experiences while considering broader conceptual understandings that inform writing and information practices. This scholarship also points to the importance of holistic pedagogical approaches that take into account the interconnected cognitive and affective domains of learning. As compositionists and instruction librarians continue to consider the intersections between our fields, we might explore further whether and how teaching writing and information literacy as interrelated can further support students in transferring their learning as they make connections between their writing and information practices.

## Reexamining Pedagogical Practices

Research on transfer, like other work on student writing and information literacy development, makes clear that these abilities progress slowly over time and not always in a linear fashion. And yet the American education system's assessment-driven environments, in which student learning is often "measured" at a single moment in time and through questions with clear-cut answers—often discourage the kind of deep learning that is vital to writing and information literacy development. Research on writing and information literacy development, including the studies explored in this chapter, illustrates that given the complexity of writing and information literacy, students need ongoing opportunities to gain practice with discrete skills and tasks, as well as with integrating those skills and applying them to various types of situations. Such learning experiences should also provide students with opportunities for feedback that helps them to reflect further on their processes. How those learning experiences are structured and presented to students is likely to have a considerable impact on how they approach writing and engaging with sources. As Jamieson and Howard argue, reading and comprehending sources is fundamental to being able to engage critically with sources and thus needs to receive far more attention in college curricula.[101] For if students do not comprehend a source or recognize its larger arguments and purposes, how can they incorporate it into their own composing in meaningful ways? This may sometimes mean that students are only asked to search for and select sources at a later point in their learning, after they have developed stronger foundational reading and analytical skills that better enable them to determine a purpose for selecting and using additional sources.

As many of the studies described in this chapter show, there is often a disconnect between how academics do research and how they teach it. The disjuncture is likely explained in part by the challenges of teaching complex tasks within constraints of a given curriculum and academic term. It is much easier, for example, to tell students simply to use peer-reviewed sources than to expect them to discern themselves whether a source is credible or not. Yet most educators ultimately want students

---

101. Jamieson and Howard, "Sentence-Mining: Uncovering the Amount of Reading and Reading Comprehension in College Writers' Researched Writing."

to be able to evaluate critically a wide range of sources, including non-scholarly information that students are more likely to encounter when they have completed their formal education.

The common gap between what students should ideally learn in college and what is stressed in coursework and assignments may call to mind recurring debates about writing and research instruction, such as whether the traditional research paper assignment has any relevance, whether students should be encouraged or dissuaded from using online sources like Wikipedia, and how to address student plagiarism. These questions can help to open productive conversations among librarians and English compositionists, and yet instead they sometimes seem to become barriers to dialogue. For example, some course instructors state that they do not assign research assignments because the products are disappointing and because use of outside sources is more likely to result in plagiarism. Others assign research assignments but advise students to locate sources only through library databases, hoping that students will then select more authoritative information.

Studies like those presented in this chapter can help composition-ists and librarians consider our pedagogies from new angles, as such research serves as a catalyst for reflection and dialogue. The sample of studies considered in this chapter make apparent the vital connections between writing and information literacy and the pedagogical value of teaching both as interrelated. Several recurring themes of these studies have particularly important implications for our teaching. These studies point to the value of pedagogical approaches such as scaffolding and inquiry-based instruction. More specifically, approaches to scaffolding can involve:

- approaching writing and information literacy development as long-term processes, in part through a reduction of instructional content and an increased use of instructional scaffolding that provides multiple opportunities for student practice and reflection and for feedback on writing and research practices;

- supporting students as developing writers, researchers, and community participants, as students build on prior knowledge and experiences, while also accepting their roles as novices who (as Sommers and Saltz might say) are writing and researching "into expertise,"[102] and

- carefully considering approaches to instructional scaffolding, in individual courses and in curricula more broadly.

Relatedly, inquiry-based teaching can:

- foreground inquiry as an exploratory, recursive, and situated process that is driven by issues that matter to real-world audiences;

- give significant attention and time to instruction on reading, comprehending, and analyzing sources, while also emphasizing the rhetorical contexts in which sources are created, distributed, and exchanged;

- represent and involve discussions about information sources as avenues through which to identify and explore questions, rather than as information containers or abstracted objects; and

- approach information systems and research tools as cultural artifacts open to rhetorical analysis, thereby challenging the conception of research technologies as neutral.

Many of these studies' pedagogical implications also have particular relevance to teaching for transfer. Such strategies include:

- presenting students with key vocabulary and concepts that assist them in understanding writing and information practices conceptually;

- inviting students to apply that vocabulary to identifying patterns in and connections between their own writing and information

---

102. Sommers and Laura Saltz, "The Novice as Expert," 134.

practices in order to develop conceptual understandings and frameworks; and

- presenting students with opportunities for reflection and meta-cognitive thinking about their experiences as developing writers, researchers, and community participants in order to foster self-directed learning and learning transfer.

These pedagogical implications are relevant not only to compositionists and librarians; they may also inform writing and information literacy instruction across subject areas.

The fact that writing and information literacy are vital to all subject areas suggests one further reason for librarian-compositionist collaboration that I have thus far given little attention: the potential for our professions to advocate for and support broader curricular changes. Compositionists and librarians' shared interests in supporting such curricular change is particularly evident in the parallels between the recently adopted ACRL *Framework for Information Literacy for Higher Education* and the WPA *Framework for Success in Postsecondary Writing* (adopted in 2011) and in the growing conversations among our professions about these documents' intersections. Often the pedagogical approaches described in the frameworks mirror the implications of the studies on writing and information literacy that have been explored in this chapter. The frameworks demonstrate ways in which both writing and information literacy can, in Charles Bazerman and David Russell's words, be experienced as "alive" and as a vital "part of human activity."[103] In the following chapter I explore these frameworks' connections and their pedagogical significance in greater detail, as I consider these documents' implications for our individual and our collaborative teaching and for building cross-professional dialogue and partnership.

---

103. Bazerman and Russell, *Writing Selves, Writing Societies*, 1.

# Chapter 3

## THE FRAMEWORKS FOR WRITING AND INFORMATION LITERACY: CATALYSTS FOR FURTHER CONVERSATION

As was explored in Chapters 1 and 2, the vital connections between writing and information literacy are evident in pedagogy centered on critical inquiry and problem-posing. Such instruction foregrounds writing and information practices as rhetorically situated activities with powerful social and communicative functions. Such an approach to writing and information literacy instruction is reflected in two key documents that in recent years have informed the work of compositionists and instruction librarians, respectively: the Council of Writing Program Administrators (WPA) *Framework for Success in Postsecondary Writing* (adopted in 2011) and the Association of College & Research Libraries (ACRL) *Framework for Information Literacy for Higher Education* (filed in 2015 and adopted in 2016). These texts (hereafter the WPA *Framework* and ACRL *Framework*) demonstrate a growing convergence between the pedagogical approaches of librarians and writing instructors, and have recently become catalysts for expanded dialogue between librarians and compositionists.

Both frameworks present alternatives to standards-based instruction as they emphasize the larger picture of why composing and information practices matter to students in their academic and personal lives. The WPA and ACRL frameworks are based on similar understandings of writing and information literacy as involving context-dependent practices that are relevant to a broad range of rhetorical situations and purposes. The frameworks also draw on pedagogical approaches that have been found to foster transfer, such as the foregrounding of interconnected conceptual understandings and frameworks, attention to learning dispositions, and metacognitive thinking. Though these texts do not explicitly discuss the issues of transfer or of teaching for it, the emphasis they place on the contextual nature of writing and information literacy, and the arguments they make that writing and information literacy education are shared responsibilities of all educators, imply transfer's importance. In this chapter I will explore the frameworks as conceptual documents that, considered together, can enrich how we, as compositionists and librarians, think about and approach writing and information pedagogies as interconnected. In other words, I will explore the WPA and ACRL frameworks as lenses through which to consider the teaching of writing and information literacy relationally, as we open further dialogue within and across our professions. In addition to analyzing intersections and overlaps between the two documents, I will also consider the WPA and ACRL frameworks' respective foci on habits of mind and conceptual understandings, and how these different emphases may function complementarily, including when teaching for transfer.

Because the connections between the WPA and ACRL frameworks are multiple and complex, this textual analysis is by no means comprehensive. Instead, it concentrates on themes that were also prominent in the preceding chapter's discussion of research on writing and information literacy development. After providing an overview of the unique origins of each document and the pedagogical philosophies and conceptual structures that shape them, I give particular attention to two especially strong qualities shared by the frameworks: 1) their emphases on rhetorically- and socially-situated inquiry and knowledge creation and 2) their attention to the diverse environments and contexts in which people engage with and create information in the twenty-first century (including in non-academic and public forums and online participatory environments). The frameworks' treatments of these two themes reflect similar conceptions of student learning and closely aligned pedagogical approaches that, according to the research on learning transfer that was discussed in Chapter 2, are likely to foster such transfer. At the same time, the documents' differing foci and structures invite professionals from both fields to consider their own work from fresh angles. Thus, the frameworks' themes reflect complementary ways that writing and information literacy education support learning within, across, and beyond academic disciplines, and both during and beyond college.

Though the scope of this chapter does not allow for an in-depth discussion of limitations and productive critiques of the frameworks, I wish to acknowledge here that neither text is perfect and that critical conversations about both documents are essential to deeper engagement with them. In concentrating here on pedagogical possibilities suggested by the frameworks, I hope to illustrate a common ground for initiating and expanding conversations between compositionists and librarians. This discussion is intended as a starting point for reflection and dialogue that can build toward further exploration of the frameworks' possibilities and limitations and toward constructive responses to them.

## Origins and Conceptual Structures of the Frameworks

The origins and conceptual structures of the WPA and ACRL frameworks reveal a great deal about the documents' pedagogical implications and they therefore provide a useful opening for a comparative analysis. In this section I will look at distinctions between each text's purposes and structures and will also consider how their attention to conceptual understandings and to the affective dimensions of learning reflect shared purposes and similarly holistic views of learning.

### The WPA Framework

The WPA *Framework*, first created in 2000 (and updated in 2008 and again in 2014), was developed as a complement to the previously established WPA *Outcomes Statement for First-Year Composition*. While the WPA *Outcomes Statement* "describes the writing knowledge, practices, and attitudes that undergraduate students develop in first-year composition,"[1] the WPA *Framework* describes habits of mind and learning experiences

---

1. Council of Writing Program Administrators, WPA *Outcomes Statement* for *First-Year Composition* (3.0), July 17, 2014, 1, http://wpacouncil.org/positions/outcomes.html.

that *prepare* students for college writing. And while the WPA *Outcomes Statement* articulates learning outcomes that are organized into four categories—Rhetorical Knowledge; Critical Thinking, Reading, and Composing; Processes; and Knowledge of Conventions—the WPA *Framework* looks beyond outcomes in order to emphasize a broader view of why writing matters in students' academic and personal lives.

The WPA *Framework*, written by both high school and college writing instructors, was furthermore intended as a means of strengthening the connections between high school and college writing curricula and was largely a response to concerns about the heavy emphasis in high school on standardized testing. The text's stress on authentic writing experiences is evident in its statement that each habit of mind should be encouraged through "writing activities and assignments [...] with genuine purposes and audiences in mind."[2] Such an approach will "foster flexibility and rhetorical versatility."[3] In contrast,

> Standardized writing curricula or assessment instruments that emphasize formulaic writing for nonauthentic audiences will not reinforce the habits of mind and the experiences necessary for success as students encounter the writing demands of postsecondary education.[4]

The WPA *Framework* consists of two main sections: 1) "Habits of Mind" and 2) "Experiences with Writing, Reading, and Critical Analysis." The eight habits of mind are defined early on in the document as "ways of approaching learning that are both intellectual and practical and that will support students' success in a variety of fields and disciplines." The learning experiences in the latter half of the document provide examples of how these habits of mind might be fostered. These learning experiences are organized into five categories, the first four of which generally correspond to the organizing categories of the WPA *Outcomes*

---

2. Council of Writing Program Administrators, National Council of Teachers of English, and National Writing Project, *Framework*, 1.

3. Ibid.

4. Ibid.

*Statement for First-Year Writing* (Rhetorical Knowledge; Critical Thinking, Reading, and Composing; Processes; and Knowledge of Conventions). The WPA *Framework* also includes an additional category for learning experiences, "Ability to Compose in Multiple Environments," which gives further attention to how both analog and digital writing tools and platforms play a role in the writing process.

Each of the WPA *Framework*'s eight habits of mind—curiosity, openness, engagement, creativity, persistence, responsibility, flexibility, and metacognition—are described early in the document, first by a definition and then through descriptions of how each habit of mind can be fostered by encouraging students to engage in certain activities. For example, the first habit of mind, curiosity, is defined as "the desire to know more about the world." Activities considered to foster curiosity include "use inquiry as a process to develop questions relevant for authentic audiences within a variety of disciplines" and "conduct research using methods for investigating questions appropriate to the discipline."[5] Though the WPA *Framework* does not indicate a conceptual origin of these "habits of mind," they share a strong resemblance to Arthur Costa and Bena Kallick's descriptions of habits of mind as described in their 2008 book, *Learning and Leading with Habits of Mind.*[6]

The latter portion of the WPA *Framework*, "Experiences with Writing, Reading, and Critical Analysis," is organized into the following five sections:

- Developing Rhetorical Knowledge
- Developing Critical Thinking
- Developing Flexible Writing Processes
- Developing Knowledge of Conventions
- Composing in Multiple Environments

---

5. Ibid., 4.

6. Arthur L. Costa and Bena Kallick, eds., *Learning and Leading with Habits of Mind: 16 Essential Characteristics for Success* (Alexandria, VA: Association for Supervision and Curriculum Development, 2008).

The learning experiences described in this latter section provide a more concrete picture of what students' actual writing activities might look like when they draw on various habits of mind. For example, "Developing Rhetorical Knowledge," defined as "the ability to analyze and act on understandings of audiences, purposes, and contexts in creating and comprehending texts," can be facilitated through activities including

- "writ[ing] for real audiences and purposes, and analyz[ing] a writer's choices in light of those audiences and purposes; and
- contribut[ing], through writing, their own ideas and opinions about a topic to an ongoing conversation."[7]

This focus on students' articulating their own perspectives through authentic writing tasks, and thereby contributing to larger discussions, is central to both the WPA and ACRL frameworks. I will return to this overarching theme again, after considering the general approach and structure of the ACRL *Framework*.

## The ACRL Framework

The ACRL *Framework* also challenges educational standardization and describes integrative pedagogical approaches, in this case through a focus on conceptual understandings. As the authors explain in the Introduction, "At the heart of this *Framework* are conceptual understandings that organize many other concepts and ideas about information, research, and scholarship into a coherent whole." This document was developed to address critiques and limitations of the ACRL *Information Literacy Standards for Higher Education*, which many librarians had argued presented an overly mechanical and simplistic view of information literacy. (ACRL had adopted the Standards in 2000. In June 2016, after developing and promoting the ACRL *Framework* as an alternative, the organization rescinded the *Standards*, to the surprise of many librarians.)

---

7. Ibid., 6.

The new framework was also intended to place a greater emphasis on the role of digital environments in locating and evaluating information, as well as on students' active roles as information creators whose work is often developed and shared in interactive environments, including online participatory platforms.[8]

The ACRL *Framework*'s divergence from a standards-based model is evident in the fact that it is intentionally called a "framework" because, as the authors explain, "it is based on a cluster of interconnected core concepts, with flexible options for implementation, rather than on a set of standards or learning outcomes, or any prescriptive enumeration of skills." This perspective is also reflected in the Introduction's definition of information literacy as "the set of integrated abilities encompassing the reflective discovery of information, the understanding of how information is produced and valued, and the use of information in creating new knowledge and participating ethically in communities of learning."

The six interrelated conceptual understandings, or "frames," that make up the majority of the ACRL *Framework* are informed by two main concepts from educational theory scholarship: 1) Grant Wiggins and Jay McTighe's approach to backward instructional design, which begins with identifying essential concepts and questions that inform a discipline, and 2) threshold concepts, defined in the *Framework* as "those ideas in any discipline that are passageways or portals to enlarged understanding or ways of thinking and practicing within that discipline."[9] These frames are:

---

8. The ACRL *Framework* initially raised heated discussions among academic librarians. This is likely due in part to how the document was first introduced by the Association of College & Research Libraries: initially the ACRL task force charged with revising the ACRL *Information Literacy Competency Standards* set out merely to update the *Standards*, but the team ultimately recommended adopting an entirely new replacement document (the *Framework*), which had a distinctly different structure. Many librarians were troubled by the perceived implications of adopting the *Framework*—namely, that they must completely overhaul their instruction programs. Relatedly, the conceptual focus of the *Framework* raised questions for many about assessment and the feasibility of using the document in their instruction programs. Recognizing these concerns, ACRL chose not to "sunset" the *Standards* immediately. For some time it was unclear what the future of the *Standards* would be.

9. Grant P. Wiggins and Jay McTighe, *Understanding by Design* (Alexandria, VA: Association for Supervision and Curriculum Development, 1998); Jan

- Authority Is Constructed and Contextual
- Information Creation as a Process
- Information Has Value
- Research as Inquiry
- Scholarship as Conversation
- Searching as Strategic Exploration

Each frame includes an explanation of the concept, which is further illustrated through related "knowledge practices" and "dispositions." The knowledge practices are defined as "demonstrations of ways in which learners can increase their understanding of these information literacy concepts." Dispositions are described as "ways in which to address the affective, attitudinal, or valuing dimension of learning." For example, the "Research as Inquiry" frame is defined as: "Research is iterative and depends upon asking increasingly complex or new questions whose answers in turn develop additional questions or lines of inquiry in any field." Its related knowledge practices include "formulate questions for research based on information gaps or on reexamination of existing, possibly conflicting, information" and "determine an appropriate scope of investigation." Among the related dispositions are "consider research as open-ended exploration and engagement with information" and "value intellectual curiosity in developing questions and learning new investigative methods." Though the larger focus of the ACRL *Framework* differs from that of the WPA *Framework*, both are clearly addressing interrelated processes and ways of thinking and approaching learning.

## Complementary Qualities: Implications for Teaching for Transfer?

While each framework reflects similar themes and pedagogical perspectives, each uses a different starting point. This is perhaps the most

Meyer, Ray Land, and Caroline Baillie, eds., *Threshold Concepts and Transformational Learning*, Educational Futures: Rethinking Theory and Practice, 42 (Rotterdam: Sense Publishers, 2010).

obvious structural difference between the WPA and ACRL frameworks: their respective foci on conceptual understandings and habits of mind. The ACRL *Framework*'s conceptual understandings are explicit articulations of overarching ideas that can help students make sense of writing and information practices conceptually; the WPA *Framework*'s habits of mind describe attitudes and approaches that foster meaningful engagement in writing and information use. Though the main structuring concepts of the two frameworks differ, their approaches share more commonalities than differences. Many of the ACRL *Framework*'s conceptual understandings are implied in the WPA *Framework*'s habits of mind and learning experiences, while the WPA *Framework*'s habits of mind and learning experiences are often mirrored in the ACRL *Framework*'s dispositions and knowledge practices. The WPA *Framework*, for instance, describes curiosity as involving "inquiry as a process to develop questions relevant for authentic audiences within a variety of disciplines"; conversely, the ACRL *Framework*'s "Research as Inquiry" dispositions articulate the importance of curiosity (e.g., "value intellectual curiosity in developing questions and learning new investigative methods").

These different ways of representing writing and information literacy can be viewed as complementary, particularly when one considers the relevance of conceptual frameworks and dispositions to learning transfer. As discussed in Chapter 2, educational research shows that key ways of fostering transfer include an emphasis on developing conceptual understandings and frameworks, metacognitive activities, and attention to affective dimensions of learning like dispositions. The frameworks repeatedly underscore these aspects of learning and thus may spark ideas about curricula that facilitate transfer. Conversely, scholarship on transfer, like that discussed in Chapter 2, offers avenues for exploring pedagogical applications of the frameworks.

Approaching the two frameworks as complementary may be particularly useful when teaching for transfer, since writing and using sources are activities that occur across contexts and that often intersect and even blur into one another. The act of gathering and analyzing information may help to contextualize writing in relation to broader conversations, at the same time that composing may help students to think more deeply about the information they encounter. The relevance of transfer to the frameworks is particularly evident in two overarching themes that they share: first, situated inquiry and knowledge creation and second, diverse information and composing environments and methods.

## Situated Inquiry and Knowledge Creation

The complementary qualities of the frameworks and their relevance to a diverse range of contexts are especially evident in their emphases on inquiry and knowledge creation. Both texts describe conceptual understandings and habits of mind that repeatedly underscore the rhe-torically-situated and social nature of writing and information practices. These two themes repeatedly intersect in each document: inquiry is nec-essary for developing new ideas, and the act of constructing knowledge inevitably leads to further questions and exploration.

As might be expected, the ACRL *Framework*, with its focus on infor-mation literacy, concentrates more heavily on the development and exploration of questions than does the WPA *Framework*, while the WPA *Framework*, with its focus on writing, places a stronger emphasis on formulating and articulating new ideas. In both documents, inquiry is presented as an iterative process of developing and exploring questions that is key to learning and to creating new knowledge. Such exploration is situated within larger social and discursive contexts, as the frameworks acknowledge that investigation and knowledge creation occur largely in and through community and dialogue. Both documents also look beyond inquiry to the act of constructing and communicating new knowledge, an activity that is highly social and dialogic and that involves both writ-ing and the use of information.

Each document portrays inquiry in similar ways, though inquiry's importance is probably made most explicit in the "Research as Inquiry" section of the ACRL *Framework*, which states, "Research is iterative and depends upon asking increasingly complex or new questions whose answers in turn develop additional questions or lines of inquiry in any field." The ability to engage in research in this way, of course, requires far more than content knowledge; perhaps more importantly it involves an acceptance of uncertainty and a curiosity and openness to explore questions. As the "Research as Inquiry" frame indicates, dispositions related to such an understanding of inquiry include:

- "consider research as open-ended exploration and engagement with information";
- "value intellectual curiosity in developing questions and learning new investigative methods"; and
- "maintain an open mind and a critical stance."

These dispositions clearly intersect with the WPA *Framework*'s descriptions of curiosity, openness, and creativity. In that text, curiosity–defined as "the desire to know more about the world"–is fostered when students are invited to:

- "use inquiry as a process to develop questions for authentic audiences [...]" and
- "conduct research using methods for investigating questions appropriate to the discipline."[10]

Openness–"the willingness to consider new ways of being and thinking in the world"–is cultivated when students:

- "practice different ways of gathering, investigating, developing, and presenting information" and
- "examine their own perspectives to find connections with the perspectives of others."[11]

---

10. Council of Writing Program Administrators, National Council of Teachers of English, and National Writing Project, WPA *Framework*, 4.

11. Ibid.

Creativity—"the ability to use novel approaches for generating, investigating, and representing ideas"—is fostered when writers are encouraged to:

- "take risks by exploring questions, topics, and ideas that are new to them" or
- "use methods that are new to them to investigate questions, topics, and ideas."[12]

All of these behaviors illustrate an approach to research that is iterative. They also intersect with ACRL *Framework* dispositions associated with "Research as Inquiry" (e.g., "value intellectual curiosity in developing questions and learning new investigative methods"; "maintain an open mind and a critical stance"). Because these interlinked conceptual understandings and habits of mind are relevant to a diverse range of composing and information tasks, they are reminders of the cross-disciplinary value of these documents and their significance when teaching for transfer.

Another key focus of the WPA and ACRL frameworks that is closely related to inquiry (and relevant across disciplines and contexts) is the act of constructing and communicating new knowledge. The theme of knowledge construction is perhaps most notable in descriptions of the social and dialogic nature of writing and of information use. Again, the ACRL *Framework* introduces this theme most directly through the conceptual understanding of "Scholarship as Conversation," while the WPA *Framework* illustrates the concept through descriptions of various habits of mind and of learning experiences that appear throughout that text.

The ACRL "Scholarship as Conversation" frame immediately calls attention to the discursive natures of research and source use:

> Research in scholarly and professional fields is a discursive practice in which ideas are formulated, debated, and weighed against one another over extended periods of time. Instead of seeking discrete answers to complex problems, experts understand that a given issue may be

---

12. Ibid., 4–5.

characterized by several competing perspectives as part of an ongoing conversation in which information users and creators come together and negotiate meaning.

This description of the dialogic quality of research, similar to the "Research as Inquiry" frame, presents inquiry as a social and ongoing process that involves openness to different views and a curiosity to explore them. Habits of mind like curiosity, openness, and engagement that are described in the WPA *Framework* are again key to such an understanding of research and scholarship as situated in relation to larger debates and conversations.

The dialogic qualities of writing and information use are further reflected in the WPA *Framework*'s descriptions of activities that foster particular habits of mind. For example, openness is cultivated when students

- "examine their own perspectives to find connections with the perspectives of others;
- practice different ways of gathering, investigating, developing, and presenting information; and
- listen to and reflect on the ideas and responses of others—both peers and instructors—to their writing."[13]

Engagement, defined as "a sense of investment and involvement in learning," is likely to occur when students

- "make connections between their own ideas and those of others;
- find meanings new to them or build on existing meanings as a result of new connections; and
- act upon the new knowledge that they have discovered." [14]

---

13. Ibid., 4.
14. Ibid.

These inquiry-based conceptions of research and writing are in sharp contrast to the view of research assignments as mere fact gathering and reporting. As discussed in Chapter 2, such a focus on writing and research as processes of engaging with and exploring larger questions and conversations encourages the kinds of inquiry-driven approaches to writing and source use that most college educators wish to encourage in their students.

## Diverse Information Environments and Inquiry Methods

In describing learning that centers on inquiry and dialogue, the WPA and ACRL frameworks give significant attention to the diverse environments, contexts, and methods through which people engage with and create information in the twenty-first century (including in non-academic and public forums and in online participatory environments). In the ACRL *Framework* the role of digital literacies is suggested to be among the central reasons for its development. The WPA *Framework*, however, gives the closest attention to the digital in its later section "Composing in Multiple Environments." Both texts describe digital technologies and online communities as offering opportunities for constructing and exchanging information with an awareness of rhetorical and social context.

The role of online environments appears more pronounced in the ACRL *Framework*, whose introduction suggests that the growth of digital information and information technologies is among the reasons that information literacy needs to be reconceptualized through this new document. The authors state that although valuable work has been done with information literacy since the publication of the ACRL *Information Literacy Competency Standards for Higher Education* in 2000, changes in information environments and in higher education "require new attention to be focused on foundational ideas about that ecosystem." The significance of digital environments is further underscored three paragraphs later when the concept of "metaliteracy" is introduced and described as an important element of the document. Metaliteracy, as explained in the

text's "Notes," "expands the scope of traditional information skills…
to include the collaborative production and sharing of information in
participatory digital environments." Such engagement with digital environments and with knowledge creation "requires an ongoing adaptation
to emerging technologies and an understanding of the critical thinking
and reflection required to engage in these spaces as producers, collabo-
rators, and distributors."[15] This emphasis on metaliteracy underscores
the importance of students as far more than information consumers.
This is a significant shift from how information literacy has tradition-
ally been conceived, a change that reflects how librarians' instructional
approaches to information literacy have become more directly connected
to the writing process.

The role of digital technologies and platforms also plays a significant role in the WPA *Framework*, though the document's introduction,
when compared to that of the ACRL *Framework*, places less stress on
the impacts of technological change on student learning. The WPA
*Framework*'s opening Executive Summary does, however, present the
document as in part a description of "twenty-first-century skills." As
stated there, "[t]his Framework describes the rhetorical and *twenty-first-
century skills* as well as habits of mind and experiences that are critical
for college success."[16]

---

15. Association of College and Research Libraries, *Framework*; Thomas
P. Mackey and Trudi Jacobson, *Metaliteracy: Reinventing Information Literacy to
Empower Learners* (Chicago: ALA Neal-Schuman, American Library Associa-
tion, 2014).

16. Council of Writing Program Administrators, National Council of Teachers of English, and National Writing Project, WPA *Framework*, 1; The lesser
degree of emphasis on technology in the WPA *Framework* (in comparison to
that in the ACRL *Framework*) may reflect differences in the historical developments of composition and library instruction. The term "information
literacy" was initially introduced in the 1970s as an articulation of the skills
needed for handling information in the technological age (and in particular
of related computer and technology skills). That emphasis has remained an
element of information literacy definitions over the decades. (See: Paul G.
Zurkowski, *The Information Service Environment Relationships and Priorities. Related
Paper No. 5,* [Washington, DC: National Program for Library and Information
Services, National Commission on Libraries and Information Science, 1974];
American Library Association, *Presidential Committee on Information Literacy:*

The significance of digital literacies to the WPA *Framework* is most pronounced in its later section "Composing in Multiple Environments," which describes "the ability to create writing using everything from traditional pen and paper to electronic technologies."[17] As with all writing, context is central to such composing. The WPA *Framework* describes the kinds of writing and reading activities in which students might engage, to include:

- "us[ing] a variety of electronic technologies intentionally to compose";
- "analyz[ing] print and electronic texts to determine how technologies affect reading and writing processes"; and
- "analyz[ing] situations where print and electronic texts are used, examining why and how people have chosen to compose using different technologies."[18]

These activities point to the complex relationships that exist between writers and the technologies they use. Relatedly, the practices reflect that composing in different environments is more than a cut-and-paste activity. Instead, writing requires careful consideration of the functionalities and the effects of various formats for fulfilling different purposes.

The ACRL and WPA frameworks address electronic environments most extensively in the document sections discussed above, but the role of the digital is apparent at numerous other points in each text. For example, the ACRL *Framework* section "Information Creation as Process" focuses on how information comes to exist in its various forms and how it is distributed and received. This frame is relevant to information created through analog modes, though the multitude of

*Final Report,* January 10, 1989, http://www.ala.org/acrl/publications/whitepapers/presidential.). In contrast, composition's historical roots are much older, and can be traced back to Greek oral tradition.

17. Council of Writing Program Administrators, National Council of Teachers of English, and National Writing Project, WPA *Framework*, 10.

18. Ibid.

digital technologies and platforms through which information is created and shared make this frame particularly relevant to digital literacies. As outlined in the document, "[i]nformation in any format is produced to convey a message and is shared via a selected delivery method. The iterative processes of researching, creating, revising, and disseminating information vary, and the resulting product reflects these differences."[19]

The relationship between information's rhetorical purposes and modes of production and distribution have important implications for both using and creating it. This is evident in knowledge practices such as:

- "articulate the capabilities and constraints of information developed through various creation processes";
- "assess the fit between an information product's creation process and a particular information need"; and
- "develop, in their own creation processes, an understanding that their choices impact the purposes for which the information product will be used and the message it conveys."[20]

Common challenges of evaluating and contextualizing online information are reflected in dispositions like:

- "accept the ambiguity surrounding the potential value of information creation expressed in emerging formats or modes"; and
- "resist the tendency to equate format with the underlying creation process."[21]

While discussion of digital literacies in the ACRL *Framework* places a stronger emphasis on information use, the WPA *Framework* gives greater attention to the creation of digital information. This is most notable in learning experiences associated with "Composing in Multiple

19. Association of College and Research Libraries, *Framework*, 5.
20. Ibid.
21. Ibid.

Environments." As with the ACRL "Information Creation as Process" frame, "Composing in Multiple Environments" does not exclude analog settings, though the text also stresses the substantial role played by digital technologies in composition.

As noted earlier, this section begins with the statement:

> Composing in multiple environments refers to the ability to create writing using everything from traditional pen and paper to electronic technologies. All forms of writing involve technologies, whether pen and paper, word processor, video recorder, or webpage. ... As electronic technologies continue to spread and evolve, writers (and teachers) need to be thoughtful, effective users who are able to adapt to changing electronic environments.[22]

Engagement in electronic environments is ideally informed by many of the same understandings of rhetoric and of writing conventions that could have been applied in the pre-Internet age. At the same time, both the WPA and the ACRL frameworks articulate particular rhetorical considerations that are in some ways unique to the digital contexts. Out of the six learning experiences listed in "Composing in Multiple Environments," four describe composing processes that involve source evaluation and use:

- analyze print and electronic texts to determine how technologies affect reading and writing;
- select, evaluate, and use information and ideas from electronic sources responsibly in their own documents (whether by citation, hotlink, commentary, or other means); [...]
- analyze situations where print and electronic texts are used, examining why and how people have chosen to compose using different technologies; and
- analyze electronic texts (their own and others') to explore and develop criteria for assessing the texts [23]

---

22. Council of Writing Program Administrators, National Council of Teachers of English, and National Writing Project, WPA *Framework*, 10.

23. Ibid.

Despite this focus on the digital, these activities are closely tied to other learning experiences outlined throughout the WPA *Framework*, like those associated with rhetorical knowledge (e.g., "write for real audiences and purposes, and analyze a writer's choices in light of those audiences and purposes"); and with knowledge of conventions (e.g., "read and analyze print and multimodal texts composed in various styles, tones, and levels of formality"). In giving substantial attention to such settings, the frameworks again convey their relevance to writing and information practices that occur in a wide range of rhetorical contexts.

## Lifelong Learning and Its Implications across the Curriculum

In stressing the wide range of contexts, environments, and communities in which writing, research, and information use occur, the frameworks offer larger views of learning that include but also extend beyond the academy. Relatedly, the understandings, abilities, and dispositions outlined in the frameworks are not things that can be mastered in a single academic term or perhaps even in an entire college career. As the WPA *Framework* asserts, "[w]riting development takes place over time as students encounter different contexts, tasks, audiences, and purposes."[24] Given that "teaching writing and learning to write are central to education and to the development of a literate citizenry," teaching college writing is not the sole responsibility of a single instructor or academic department; rather, it "is shared by teachers, schools, students, and families."[25]

Similarly, the ACRL *Framework* "envisions information literacy as extending the arc of learning throughout students' academic careers and as converging with other academic and social learning goals." Thus, the ACRL *Framework* "is not designed to be implemented in a single information literacy session in a student's academic career; it is intended to be developmentally and systematically integrated into the student's academic program at a variety of levels." Information literacy development

---

24. Ibid., 2.
25. Ibid., 3.

is therefore presented as a joint responsibility of students, teaching faculty, and librarians across content areas. As the ACRL *Framework*'s introduction states,

> Students have a greater role and responsibility in creating new knowledge, in understanding the contours and the changing dynamics of the world of information, and in using information, data, and scholarship ethically. Teaching faculty have a greater responsibility in designing curricula and assignments that foster enhanced engagement with the core ideas about information and scholarship within their disciplines. Librarians have a greater responsibility in identifying core ideas within their own knowledge domain that can extend learning for students, in creating a new cohesive curriculum for information literacy, and in collaborating more extensively with faculty.[26]

As the frameworks emphasize writing and information literacy as context-dependent abilities that are not learned quickly but rather must be integrated across curricula and learning contexts, they illustrate their relevance across and beyond academic disciplines.

This again suggests the relevance of transfer to both documents, even though neither explicitly mentions this concept. The fact that both texts also describe specific activities that, according to the transfer research, may help students to apply their learning across contexts (namely, developing conceptual understandings, reflective dispositions, and metacognition), further implies the value of these documents to teaching across the curriculum. As noted earlier in this chapter, approaching the frameworks as complementary texts may help to open further exploration of how integrated approaches to teaching writing and information literacy can foster transfer.

As I have considered throughout this chapter, although the structures of each document and the impulses to create them are distinct, both represent writing and information literacy as socially situated while also describing them as abilities that develop and evolve throughout one's life. The frameworks illustrate that composing and information practices, to

---

26. Association of College and Research Libraries, *Framework*, 2.

use Christine Pawley's words, "never stand[] alone" and are "always produced and used in ways that represent social relationships."[27] Moreover,
with their emphases on students as constructors of new knowledge,
the frameworks reflect the statement of Charles Bazerman and David
Russell that "[w]riting is alive when it is being written, read, remembered, contemplated, followed—when it is part of human activity."[28] In
describing inquiry and knowledge creation as occurring through active
participation in discourse communities and engagement in a diverse
range of environments (both analog and digital), the frameworks relate
student work to real-world experiences and audiences. In acknowledging
how expanding digital environments have affected writing and information environments and practices, these documents also enable broader
conceptions of "writing" and "information literacy" than those evoked
by traditional scholarly models of academic writing and research.

## New Vocabularies for Cross-Disciplinary Dialogue

The value of the WPA and ACRL frameworks to compositionists
and librarians comes in large part because they offer new vocabularies
for talking and thinking about composing and information practices as
interconnected. This new language may help to address many of the
barriers that have stood between gaining deeper understandings of
one another's professions and instructional approaches. The intersections between writing, research, and information use have been familiar
to many compositionists and librarians for some time, but we have
sometimes struggled to find a common language for talking across our
professional communities about these connections. The remarkably
similar language and pedagogical approaches outlined in the frameworks,
however, reflect a growing convergence in the ways that many writing

---

27. Christine Pawley, "Information Literacy: A Contradictory Coupling,"
*Library Quarterly* 73, no. 4 (2003): 425.

28. Charles Bazerman and David R. Russell, eds., *Writing Selves, Writing Societies: Research from Activity Perspectives*, Perspectives on Writing, an Electronic
Books Series (Fort Collins, CO: WAC Clearinghouse, 2003), 1.

instructors and librarians conceive of teaching and learning. This includes how we envision our instructional work within the broader context of higher education and suggests that those visions may be more aligned than we have often recognized.

This is particularly interesting in light of professional literature that indicates a long-existing disconnect between common pedagogical approaches in English composition and in library instruction.[29] With growing discussion between librarians and compositionists, our professions appear increasingly better positioned to collaborate in fuller and more meaningful ways. Those interested in reading more about compositionists' and librarians' thoughts on and work with the connections between the frameworks may be interested in the recently published book *The Future Scholar: Researching & Teaching the Frameworks for Writing & Information Literacy*.[30] The subsequent chapter on collaborations between compositionists and librarians offers further consideration of the possibilities for applying ideas articulated in the WPA and ACRL frameworks to compositionists' and librarians' actual teaching practices, as we recognize and articulate the deep connections between

---

29. Grace L. Veach, "Tracing Boundaries, Effacing Boundaries: Information Literacy as an Academic Discipline" (Ph.D. dissertation, University of Southern Florida, 2012), http://scholarcommons.usf.edu/cgi/viewcontent. cgi?article=5609&context=etd; Rolf Norgaard, "Writing Information Literacy: Contributions to a Concept," *Reference & User Services Quarterly* 43, no. 2 (Winter 2003): 124–30; Donna Mazziotti and Teresa Grettano, "'Hanging Together': Collaboration between Information Literacy and Writing Programs Based on the ACRL Standards and the WPA Outcomes," in *ACRL 2011 Conference Papers* (Chicago: Association of College & Research Libraries, 2011), 180–90, http://www.ala.org/acrl/sites/ala.org.acrl/files/content/ conferences/confsandpreconfs/national/2011/papers/hanging_together. pdf; James K. Elmborg, "Locating the Center: Libraries, Writing Centers, and Information Literacy," *The Writing Lab Newsletter* 30, no. 6 (2006): 7–11; Melissa Bowles-Terry, Erin Davis, and Wendy Holliday, "'Writing Information Literacy' Revisited: Application of Theory to Practice in the Classroom," *Reference & User Services Quarterly* 49, no. 3 (2010): 225–30; Celia Rabinowitz, "Working in a Vacuum: A Study of the Literature of Student Research and Writing," *Research Strategies* 17, no. 4 (January 4, 2000): 337–46, doi:10.1016/ S0734-3310(01)00052-0.

30. Randall McClure and James P. Purdy, eds., *The Future Scholar: Researching & Teaching the Frameworks for Writing and Information Literacy* (Medford, NJ: Information Today, 2016).

writing and information literacy and as we reexamine the possibilities for collaboration.

# Chapter 4

## COMPOSITION-LIBRARY COLLABORATIONS: NOTES FROM THE FIELDS

The WPA *Framework for Success in Postsecondary Writing* and the ACRL *Framework for Information Literacy for Higher Education*,[1] explored in depth in the previous chapter, have provoked productive questions within and across the English composition and library professions about how we approach education as a shared responsibility of all educators. These documents illustrate that writing and information literacy education must be collaborative efforts that are pursued within and beyond university writing programs. Partnerships between librarians and compositionists can be powerful, not only for compositionists' and librarians' own direct teaching, but also for expanding broader curricular efforts across the disciplines.

Collaborations among compositionists and librarians are, of course, by no means new. Cross-pollination between these professions has been occurring to varying degrees for decades, and has grown considerably since the ACRL's adoption of the *Information Literacy Competency Standards for Information Literacy for Higher Education* in 2000. Such work appears to be gaining momentum in the past several years, in particular since the filing of the ACRL *Framework* in February 2015 and its subsequent adoption

---

1. Council of Writing Program Administrators, National Council of Teachers of English, and National Writing Project, *Framework for Success in Postsecondary Writing*, 2011, http://wpacouncil.org/files/framework-for-success-postsecondary-writing.pdf; Association of College and Research Libraries, *Framework for Information Literacy for Higher Education*, 2015, http://www.ala.org/acrl/standards/ilframework.

in February 2016. The potential for growing library-writing program partnerships appears especially ripe now. Librarians are increasingly centering their instruction on problem-posing and on the rhetorical purposes of information use in various contexts. At the same time, writing programs are placing a greater emphasis on digital literacies, multimodal writing, and participation in a broad range of writing environments that require deeper engagement with information literacy. Such instructional approaches require that students evaluate and make strategic use of a wide variety of sources as they situate their own ideas in relation to those of others.

Collaborations are increasing not only in number, but also often in intensity: many involve deeper conversations about effective pedagogy and many extend far beyond library "add-ons" like supplementary course materials or a single library session. These partnerships also frequently involve considerations of the intersections between writing and information literacy that inform course learning outcomes, class activities, sequenced assignments, course materials, and class instruction. Though such extensive collaboration is still far from the norm, something is shifting in how our professions understand one another's work. With that shift, the opportunities for fuller partnership multiply.

While the possibilities for collaboration are great, so too are the challenges. When people have a finite amount of time, energy, and resources, and often feel overworked, how do they invest the efforts needed to build meaningful partnerships, let alone find the motivation to do so? Having personally struggled as a librarian to build fuller collaborations with writing programs, I wanted to explore from an interpersonal perspective how extensive library-writing program relationships come to exist and how they are sustained. What kinds of environments and conditions foster this kind of joint work? What benefits do librarians and compositionists who partner with one another more extensively see in their shared work? What are these partners able to accomplish together that they could not accomplish alone? What challenges arise for librarians and compositionists who work closely together, and how do they respond to those difficulties?

In this and the subsequent chapter I consider the possibilities for and the challenges of building fuller compositionist-librarian partnerships through several lenses. In this chapter, I concentrate on the personal and interpersonal experiences of several composition-library partners who generously agreed to be interviewed about their collaborations. In Chapter 5, I widen the lens to consider composition-library collaborations in relation to the historical and structural contexts that have greatly influenced the instructional and institutional roles of both librarians and compositionists. There I first consider the similar historical developments of writing and library instruction and their potential implications for library-writing program partnerships. This historical context provides a background for further exploring the interpersonal dimensions of such alliances in relation to the institutional and professional cultures in which compositionists and librarians work. Chapters 4 and 5 are informed largely by professional literature from both fields, and in particular by literature on the sociocultural and psychological dimensions of faculty-librarian relations, work that has significant implications for cultivating meaningful teaching partnerships.

While the interviews described in this chapter provide concrete examples of various ways that our professions can work together and the benefits and challenges of this joint work, the historical and sociocultural contexts considered in the next chapter offer a broader perspective from which to view the possibilities and challenges of collaboration in our various teaching environments and institutions. My hope is that in identifying both connections and disconnects that sometimes occur between individuals in our fields, and in considering these in relation to interpersonal, sociocultural, and environmental conditions, compositionists and librarians may view our individual and our shared teaching practices from new angles. These perspectives help us to reflect in particular on assumptions and preconceptions about writing or library instruction that may sometimes limit the potential for dialogue across professional lines. Such a perspective can help us to expand conversations and alliances that involve increasingly more individuals in our professions.

## Interviewing Approach and Process

When I first set out to write this book I had not planned to conduct the interviews that inform this chapter. But in the process of writing the value of such conversations became obvious. Having engaged only in less extensive collaborations with writing instructors, having read an extensive amount of scholarship on library-composition partnerships, and having previously taught college writing, I felt like I was missing a deeper view of librarians' and compositionists' experiences with more involved partnerships, including the interpersonal dimensions of such interactions. Since relationships are at the heart of collaboration, and since academic literature often does not adequately address these relational dimensions, I believed that this book would be enriched if I were able to share the perspectives of other librarians and compositionists, in addition to my own experiences and viewpoints.

Reflecting on my questions about the possibilities for (and the obstacles to) fuller partnerships, I sought to learn more about the experiences and viewpoints of compositionists and librarians who have engaged in more extensive collaborations. Semi-structured, conversational interviews would offer a means for hearing about aspects of individuals' experiences that usually receive less attention in the professional literature of both fields. I therefore reached out to four pairs of librarian-compositionist partners who have built and sustained long-term collaborations, informed them about my book project and the purpose of the interviews, and asked if they would be available for a conversation about their joint efforts. I had learned of these projects through professional library conferences and recent library literature and felt that each partnership stood out because each individual exhibited strong mutual engagement and investment in teaching writing and information literacy as interconnected.

The individuals I approached shared their experiences in recorded interviews. Each interview involved three people: a compositionist, a librarian, and me. These discussions enabled me to identify themes and differences in interviewees' experiences and to gain a more personal view of the various partnerships. The projects that are discussed here were chosen because of the considerable engagement that each individual brings to the work; the long-term goals and distinct designs and approaches of their projects; and the varied instructional environments and institutional contexts in which these individuals work. I chose to limit the number of interviews I conducted in order to provide a more focused discussion of the contexts and experiences of each collaboration.

Because I did not view the eight interviewees as "subjects," but rather as colleagues with a shared interest, I approached the interviews as informal (albeit professional) conversations, rather than as a formal research study. I therefore did not seek Institutional Review Board (IRB) approval, but I did ask interviewees for permission to record them. I also informed interviewees that prior to submitting my book manuscript I would request that they review my descriptions of their work and of our conversations. I wanted to ensure that what was published accurately reflected their experiences and perspectives and that they were comfortable with having this information appear in print. Thus, the information reported in this book appears with the consent of these interviewees. I am grateful to all of these individuals for taking the time to share openly about their experiences, their particular approaches to "writing information literacy," and their views of and responses to obstacles that can stand in the way of more integrative approaches to teaching about writing, research, and information use.

As noted previously, I approached these interviews with particular interest in the following questions:

- How do such partnerships come to exist? What conditions enable these collaborations to develop and to be sustained?
- What do librarians and compositionists perceive to be the benefits of collaboration? What are these librarians and compositionists able to accomplish together that they could not do alone?
- What stands in the way of meaningful partnerships, and how do these individuals respond to those difficulties?

To explore these questions, I asked interviewees about how their partnerships have developed and evolved; the unique experiences, knowledge, and perspectives that each brings to their joint initiatives; and successes and challenges of their collaborative work, much of which aims to effect curricular and institutional change. At the beginning of our conversations, I articulated these broader points of inquiry to the interviewees and explained that I was approaching the interviews as conversations. Though I had specific question prompts on hand, usually discussions led naturally to addressing the broader questions I had identified.

Although most of the partnerships described here have involved more than one project, each has had a recent major undertaking that is particularly illustrative of the given collaboration and its pedagogical implications. This chapter concentrates in part on those projects, while also exploring the interviewees' overall collaborative experiences. By describing how collaboration has influenced their own direct teaching and their broader pedagogical efforts, the interviewees illustrate how the experience and knowledge of librarians and compositionists can function complementarily.

## Partnerships: Overviews

Each of the collaborations explored in these interviews primarily involves one librarian and one compositionist. In all cases, however, the interviewees' projects aim to strengthen the connections between a much larger number of librarian and composition colleagues. Each partnership takes a different form and is influenced by their distinct environments and circumstances, but all involve far more than a quick overview of library resources and services or of search mechanics. These relationships are founded on the understanding that writing and information literacy are intertwined, and on the shared goal of fostering student engagement in genuine inquiry, critical dialogue, and ultimately knowledge creation. Their success might be explained largely by the interviewees' shared goals, appreciation for one another's expertise, and a grass-roots approach that is sensitive to the local environment, institutional culture, and community members. The interviewees' experiences illustrate how the unique expertise of librarians and compositionists can function in a complementary fashion, enriching the interviewees' own direct teaching as well as their broader efforts to make writing and information literacy integral to learning across the disciplines.

At the University of Colorado-Boulder (UCB), Michelle Albert, compositionist and Information Literacy Coordinator for the UCB Program for Writing and Rhetoric (PWR), and Caroline Sinkinson, Instruction Coordinator/Reference Librarian for Research and Instructional Services, discussed their long-term work with the PWR and their recent development of an information literacy curriculum for first-year writing there. These materials draw heavily on concepts and pedagogical approaches articulated in both the ACRL *Framework* and the WPA *Framework*. At the University of Scranton, Director of First-Year Writing Teresa Grettano and Public Services Librarian Donna Witek discussed their joint work since 2009, which has included co-teaching, initiating conversations and curricular planning for first-year writing among writing instructors and librarians, and analyzing documents like the WPA and ACRL frameworks in order to articulate connections and complements between them that may help to open further dialogue. At Hunter College, first-year composition program director Wendy Hayden and instructional design librarian Stephanie Margolin described their growing collaboration, which led them to create the Research Toolkit, an online resource (library.hunter.cuny.edu/research-toolkit) for faculty teaching writing- and research-intensive courses. This resource includes instruction materials that take an inquiry-based approach to the research process. At the University of Vermont, Writing in the Disciplines Program Director Susanmarie Harrington and Reference and Instruction Librarian Dan DeSanto discussed their institution's initiative Writing and Information Literacy in the Disciplines (WILD), which supports departments and faculty in developing program curricula that approach writing and information literacy as inseparable and as vital to student learning. To help contextualize the major themes that organize this chapter and the larger questions that drove the interviews, I will first provide further description of each partnership.

*University of Colorado-Boulder: Integrating the WPA & ACRL Frameworks into Composition Curricula*

Michelle Albert and Caroline Sinkinson's work at the University of Colorado-Boulder is a reminder of the potential that the WPA and ACRL frameworks present for deepening the connections between writing and information literacy instruction. Working at a public research institution with about 32,000 enrolled students (including about 26,000 undergraduates), Michelle and Caroline have integrated concepts and language from both frameworks in order to propose a new information literacy curriculum for their First-Year Writing course that includes a theoretical frame, learning outcomes, and activities, and to which more extensive materials will be added. Since this First-Year Writing course includes about 120 sections each semester, the potential impact of this work is significant.

Michelle and Caroline's integration of the WPA and ACRL frameworks illustrates the potential for aligning the two documents to inform curricular design and to open cross-professional dialogue. In their 2015 conference presentation, "Composing Information Literacy," Michelle and Caroline introduce their proposed First-Year Writing information literacy curriculum by first posing the question: "If we could design a curriculum that no longer treats Information Literacy and Rhetoric and Composition as separate, and that acknowledges the complex information landscapes in which we reside and the multiple modes in which our students compose, what would it look like?"[2] They then go on to explore the intersections between the frameworks and their reenvisioning of a

---

2. Michelle Albert and Caroline Sinkinson, "Composing Information Literacy: A Pedagogical Partnership Between Rhet/Comp and Library Faculty" (Georgia International Conference on Information Literacy, Savannah, Georgia, September 25, 2015), http://digitalcommons.georgiasouthern.edu/gaintlit/2015/2015/74/.

first-year writing curriculum that gives greater attention to information and digital literacies. Integrating ideas from both frameworks (the ACRL *Framework*'s conceptual understandings and WPA *Framework*'s habits of mind and learning experiences), they developed six categories/themes for articulating instructional content, outcomes, and activities:

- Inquiry & Scholarship as Dialogic
- Agency & Flexibility in a Messy Process
- Engagement - Participation & Responsibility
- Context - Authority & Genre
- Metacognition - Reflection & Transfer
- Environments - New & Emerging

Michelle and Caroline have written in greater detail about this work in their recently published book chapter "Composing Information Literacy through Pedagogical Partnerships."[3]

Michelle and Caroline have introduced their theories and instructional materials to PWR faculty, and will be meeting with a focus group of writing instructor colleagues to solicit specific feedback on their work. At the time of this writing (spring 2016) they are further developing course materials that will be implemented and assessed in a first-year writing course. Their experiences with these materials will open further conversation with other writing instructors.

This project was inspired by engagement with the Program for Writing and Rhetoric's Digital Composition Committee, which promotes giving greater attention to digital literacies (including the ways in which they intersect with information literacy). The PWR's investment in information literacy is further evident in its long-standing work with UCB's libraries, the First-Year Writing program's emphasis on information

---

3. Michelle Albert and Caroline Sinkinson, "Composing Information Literacy through Pedagogical Partnerships," in *The Future Scholar: Researching & Teaching the Frameworks for Writing and Information Literacy*, ed. Randall McClure and James P. Purdy (Medford, NJ: Information Today, 2016), 111–29.

literacy, and Michelle's role as PWR Information Literacy Coordinator, a title that reflects the program's teaching priorities and values.

## University of Scranton: Evolving Pedagogies through Co-Teaching, Dialogue, and Analysis of Professional Documents

Teresa Grettano and Donna Witek, working at the University of Scranton, a private Jesuit university with about 6,000 enrolled students (including about 4,000 undergraduates), have similarly found documents like the WPA and ACRL frameworks to be powerful means for opening conversations across the professions and establishing foundations for curricular development. Like Michelle and Caroline, Teresa and Donna have a long-standing partnership that has involved a variety of projects, including the development of curricular materials for a first-year writing program, in part through conversations about professional documents like the WPA and ACRL frameworks.

Teresa and Donna's partnership began in 2009 when Teresa received one of the institution's Information Literacy Stipends, which support faculty in integrating information literacy into a course through collaboration with a librarian. During that academic year, Teresa and Donna developed a course on rhetoric and social media that focused specifically on Facebook. In spring 2011 they co-taught this course for the first time.[4] This course development project served as a foundation for their extensive work in comparing official documents from composition and librarianship that articulate pedagogical goals and approaches. For example, their 2011 conference presentation "Hanging Together": Collaboration between Information Literacy and Writing Programs Based on the ACRL *Standards* and the WPA *Outcomes*" is a comparative analysis of two key documents (the WPA *Outcomes Statement for*

---

4. For a more detailed discussion of the co-taught course see: Donna Witek and Teresa Grettano, "Teaching Metaliteracy: A New Paradigm in Action," *Reference Services Review* 42, no. 2 (2014): 188–208; Donna Witek and Teresa Grettano, "Revising for Metaliteracy: Flexible Course Design to Support Social Media Pedagogy," in *Metaliteracy in Practice*, ed. Trudi E. Jacobson and Thomas P. Mackey (Chicago: Neal-Schuman Publishers, 2015), 1–22.

*First-Year Writing* and the ACRL *Information Literacy Competency Standards for Higher Education*) used in the professions to inform teaching. Teresa and Donna's more recent analyses of the connections and distinctions between the WPA and ACRL frameworks build on this earlier work.[5] This textual analysis has provided material for opening conversations between first-year writing instructors and librarians and for developing a first-year writing curriculum that foregrounds information literacy.

## *Hunter College: A Research Toolkit as a Beginning for Advocacy*

Hunter College is the largest college of the City University of New York (CUNY), with over 23,000 students and about 17,000 undergraduates. There, Wendy Hayden and Stephanie Margolin have created the "Research Toolkit," an online resource providing instructional materials that encourage inquiry-based approaches to writing and information literacy instruction (library.hunter.cuny.edu/research-toolkit). As they describe in their article "Beyond Mechanics," the toolkit is a means of advocacy that invites both students and faculty "to think beyond mechanics, beyond a checklist mentality." The toolkit recasts the goal of information literacy instruction as "not about finding the 'correct' sources, but about the development of ideas-emphasizing inquiry, reading, and synthesis."[6]

Wendy and Stephanie were initially introduced to one another and asked to jointly develop and facilitate a faculty workshop on the role of the research paper in the curriculum. They quickly recognized the

---

5. Donna Mazziotti and Teresa Grettano, "'Hanging Together': Collaboration between Information Literacy and Writing Programs Based on the ACRL Standards and the WPA Outcomes," in ACRL 2011 *Conference Papers* (Association of College & Research Libraries Annual Conference, Philadelphia, PA, 2011), 180–90, http://www.ala.org/acrl/sites/ala.org.acrl/files/content/conferences/confsandpreconfs/national/2011/papers/hanging_together.pdf.

6. Stephanie Margolin and Wendy Hayden, "Beyond Mechanics: Reframing the Pedagogy and Development of Information Literacy Teaching Tools," *Journal of Academic Librarianship* 41, no. 5 (2015): 610, doi:10.1016/j.acalib.2015.07.001.

connections between their fields, interests, and pedagogical approaches and began to learn more about the work and literature in one another's professions. Ultimately, they created the toolkit as a means of support for instructors across campus who were teaching writing and information practices and encouraging inquiry-driven approaches to learning. Soon after the toolkit's completion, Wendy became coordinator of the first-year writing course, which has enabled her to promote the kinds of instructional approaches reflected in the Research Toolkit. At the same time, librarians have begun extending their teaching involvement beyond one-shot instruction to sequenced instruction and collaborative assignment design.

## University of Vermont: The Writing and Information Literacy in the Disciplines Program

At the University of Vermont, a land-grant and research institution with a total enrollment of about 13,000 (and about 11,000 undergraduates), Susanmarie Harrington and Dan DeSanto have partnered in the Writing and Information Literacy in the Disciplines (WILD) initiative, which brings together disciplinary faculty, writing faculty, and librarians to reenvision discipline-specific program curricula. WILD grew out of an initiative of the university's General Education Committee to make writing and information literacy central parts of the curriculum. Previously, the university did not have a writing course requirement and writing and information literacy had not been systematically emphasized across campus. While UVM's programmatic integration of both writing and information literacy is unique, the WILD program foundations are greatly informed by the University of Minnesota's Writing Enhanced Curriculum initiative.

WILD takes a grassroots approach to program development that works to avoid negative perceptions of administrative mandates. The WILD website states four main outcomes for departments:

1. identifying disciplinary priorities for writing and information literacy
2. developing student outcomes based on these priorities
3. creating a departmental curriculum map of where the outcomes are taught, and
4. constructing a plan for assessing and refining outcomes [7]

This process also involves examining writing assignments and developing sequenced instruction that enable progressive development of information literacy.

The exact approach that any department takes to this process depends on contextual factors like existing relationships and department priorities. Generally speaking, compositionists from the Writing in the Disciplines program serve as the main facilitators, librarians lend their knowledge and experience to furthering conversations about the roles of research and information use in the academic program, and department liaisons (also members of the given department) play a particularly active role in engaging faculty in their programs in the planning process. The WILD initiative is particularly useful in considering the potential for compositionists and librarians to advocate for broader curricular initiatives that bring together educators across disciplines.

While the specific circumstances in which all four of these partnerships have developed vary, they all reflect important conditions needed for meaningful collaboration. As suggested above, perhaps most important are a recognition of shared goals and a mutual appreciation for each partner's expertise. Such conditions were most evident when interviewees saw specific opportunities to work jointly and found commonalities between their teaching and their pedagogical philosophies. Moreover, these partners' sensitivity and responsiveness to their local environments and communities reflect creative and unique approaches that may help other educators generate fresh ideas for their own contexts.

---

7. Writing in the Disciplines Program, University of Vermont, "Writing & Information Literacy in the Disciplines (WILD)," 2016, https://www.uvm. edu/wid/?Page=partners.html.

## Establishing and Sustaining Partnerships

Given the challenges of establishing and continuing such involved collaborations, I was curious to know how these projects began and what has carried them forward. Because environment and institutional culture can play such a strong role in the nature of a teaching partnership, it was important to me to learn about the various kinds of collaborations, including the different forms that they take, the different types of institutions in which they have developed, and the varying lengths of time for which they have been in place. It is useful to keep in mind the range of contexts in which each of these partnerships has developed and the unique possibilities and challenges that each presents. At the same time, all of these collaborations reflect the fact that relationships need time to develop and are much more likely to be sustained when individuals have the time and institutional support that enables an ongoing exchange and development of ideas. The interviewees' reported experiences support Ruth Ivey's conclusion, based on interviews with librarian-faculty partners, that successful partnerships are characterized by: both parties having a shared and understood goal; mutual respect, tolerance, and trust; competence for the task at hand; and engagement in ongoing dialogue.[8]

Several prominent themes recurred throughout the interviewees' descriptions of conditions that were key to initiating and continuing their partnerships. Perhaps most important were shared goals, mutual appreciation for one another's expertise, and an openness to one another's ideas, all of which were vital to sustaining these connections. Because this theme was also prominent in the interviewees' perceptions of the benefits of collaboration, it is discussed in greater depth in this chapter's next section. Serendipity and circumstance played significant roles in whether and how partnerships started and grew, as did the degree of institutional and programmatic support provided for these collaborative

---

8. Ruth Ivey, "Information Literacy: How Do Librarians and Academics Work in Partnership to Deliver Effective Learning Programs?", *Australian Academic & Research Libraries* 34, no. 2 (June 2003): 102.

initiatives. Whether or not close collaboration between a campus's library and writing program had occurred previously also played an influential role in the nature of these partnerships. Two of the four collaborations grew out of long-standing connections between a library and a writing program (Michelle and Caroline's work at the University of Colorado-Boulder and Susanmarie and Dan's at the University of Vermont). In the other two instances (Teresa and Donna's efforts at the University of Scranton and Wendy and Stephanie's at Hunter College), the partners' joint efforts have been openings for building stronger relationships between librarians and writing teachers. While on a previously established connection may benefit from other existing supports, its absence may also be an opportunity to explore new ways of working collectively that might otherwise be more difficult to recognize.

Particularly in the case of newly established library-writing program connections, interviewees often described their partnerships as largely the result of "a lot of serendipity and a lot of circumstance," as Stephanie commented. For example, Stephanie and Wendy became acquainted through a colleague who asked them to do a joint workshop series on teaching the research paper. Because of that experience, the two recognized their shared interests and pedagogical approaches and the strong connections between their work. When the workshop series had a low turnout, the two decided to develop the Research Toolkit (described earlier in this chapter). As Stephanie noted, if the workshops hadn't been given or had been better attended, they might not have been motivated to create the toolkit, which has been a catalyst for further collaboration and for their broader engagement with other writing instructors and librarians.

Similarly, Teresa and Donna's relationship can also be attributed largely to serendipity. Before they became involved, the library and writing program interactions had consisted of one-shot library sessions and limited dialogue (even though the Dean of the library taught in the First-Year Writing program). Teresa and Donna became acquainted soon after Teresa joined the University of Scranton, when she learned about the library's Information Literacy Stipends at a new faculty orientation.

These funds support teaching-faculty instructors in integrating information literacy into a course through collaboration with a librarian. Interested in developing a new course on social media literacy and Facebook, Teresa contacted the library and was referred to Donna, the subject librarian for English. Prior to then, Teresa had little knowledge of the instructional work that librarians do and was unaware of documents like the ACRL *Information Literacy Competency Standards* (which prior to the filing of the ACRL *Framework* was the main resource academic librarians across institutions used to define information literacy). Despite not yet having this knowledge of academic librarianship, Teresa came to the partnership eager for Donna's input on the course and open to learning from a librarian's perspective. By developing the course together, the two discovered powerful connections between their instructional work and professions, which ultimately led to their extensive work on the intersections between writing and information literacy.

The other two collaborations—Caroline and Michelle's work at the University of Colorado-Boulder Program for Writing and Rhetoric and Susanmarie and Dan's efforts with the University of Vermont's Writing and Information Literacy in the Disciplines Program—developed out of previously established alliances related respectively to First-Year Composition and to the General Education curriculum and initiatives. In both of these instances, curriculum committees in which both librarians and compositionists played key roles served as forums for people to discuss shared goals and to explore possible strategies for working toward those goals. These connections provided a stronger foundation upon which to extend those conversations to other campus partners.

For example, Susanmarie and Dan's engagement with the WILD initiative builds on earlier General Education Committee work at a time when there was neither a campus-wide writing course nor campus-wide learning outcomes for writing or information literacy. At that time, Susanmarie and another librarian on the General Education Committee recognized that the overlaps between writing and information literacy could help to simplify general education learning outcomes and address learning goals shared across campus. This advocacy on the committee led to the implementation of the Foundational Writing and Information Literacy program in 2014, which implements a set of writing and information literacy outcomes across three first-year courses, in an effort to reach nearly every first-year student. The establishment of that course provided faculty with a context in which the goals of the WILD program could be better understood and appreciated.

Caroline and Michelle have similarly benefited from a long-standing relationship between their campus writing program and the libraries, a connection that comes with programmatic supports. They expressed appreciation for the fact that the Program for Writing and Rhetoric prioritizes information literacy in tangible ways, including the funding for Michelle's work as the PWR's Information Literacy Coordinator. This prioritizing is largely a result of more than a decade of mutual engagement, in which librarians have listened to, examined, and developed tailored responses to the PWR program's needs, while PWR advocates like Michelle and her predecessor have helped initiate and facilitate conversations and efforts. In addition to this, the current PWR director has articulated his interest in building the program's emphasis on information literacy, in particular as it intersects with digital literacy. Significant efforts and resources have been devoted to fulfilling this goal, such as the formation of an ad-hoc Digital Composition Leaders Committee that examined implications of digital literacy for the PWR curriculum. It was that committee's work which prompted Michelle and Caroline, who have collaborated extensively over the years, to reenvision the First-Year Writing curriculum in relation to the WPA and ACRL frameworks.

As this reflects, institutional support in various forms was another important factor that enabled these connections to grow. For example, Michelle's position as Information Literacy Coordinator in her Program for Writing and Rhetoric involves one course release per year that allows time for her to deliberately engage with information literacy integration. Similarly, the WILD program has been feasible largely because Susanmarie and Dan are given time and resources to devote to the project. However, the amount of time that participants give to WILD can be tricky to balance along with other responsibilities, and because WILD is supported by an outside grant and not by internal funding, the potential for sustaining the program beyond the grant funding period is uncertain.

## Benefits of Collaboration and Complementary Partner Roles

Given that these partnerships require considerable amounts of time and energy, I wanted to know more about what makes them worthwhile to the interviewees. What are these compositionists and librarians able to accomplish together that they could not accomplish if they only worked with colleagues within their own profession? Relatedly, how might librarians' and compositionists' knowledge, experience, or institutional positioning function in complementary ways? Interestingly, most interviewees responded to these questions with a thoughtful pause, followed by the statement, "That's a really interesting question." While individuals clearly valued the benefits of working with someone from another profession who had a different viewpoint on teaching and learning and on their institution, most people apparently had not previously articulated how their work functioned complementarily. This may be a reflection of the fact that conversations among the professions more generally have been limited. When such relationships develop between just two individuals, they are perhaps unlikely to explicitly discuss how each brings something unique to their work.

Despite interviewees' initial pause upon being asked how their work functions in complementary ways, they ultimately had a great deal to say about this. Common themes of those responses were:

- **subject and professional expertise:** appreciation for one another's distinct expertise and perspectives on student learning, which are informed by differing kinds of relationships to and interactions with students;
- **expanding pedagogical perspectives:** cross-professional dialogue that expanded interviewees' own perspectives on teaching and learning; and

- **institutional positions:** the benefits of working jointly while occupying different positions and roles in relation to academic programs and institutions

As these themes suggest, partners found that their joint work enabled them to consider their own teaching from new angles and to advocate for writing and information literacy education on a larger programmatic level.

## Subject and Professional Expertise

Compositionists' and librarians' knowledge and teaching experiences repeatedly appeared to function complementarily. While compositionists generally possessed more subject expertise in composition and rhetoric, librarians had deep understandings of information systems and environments and of information-seeking behaviors. Some librarians had also become relatively well-versed in composition and rhetoric literature because of their own independent reading and their own engagement with library literature that underscores writing-information literacy connections (such as work by James Elmborg, Barbara Fister, and Rolf Norgaard). Librarians brought a cross-disciplinary lens to their work and a unique knowledge of how students struggle with locating and evaluating sources, while writing instructors usually had more extensive classroom experience with teaching credit-bearing courses and with curriculum design and learning assessment. Relatedly, librarians commented on writing instructors' more extended class time with students, which presented more opportunities for student learning than is possible during a single library session.

Librarians, on the other hand, may have a fuller understanding of the ways students search for and select information sources, in part because of librarians' interactions with students at the reference desk and during class sessions. As Susanmarie commented, while compositionists generally have more in-depth experience with curricular design and assessment, librarians have more experience with the actual lived experience of the curriculum, with what students do when doing an assignment, as in "I'm in the library working on my paper, or assignment." Most faculty imagine what that process is like, but librarians are actually in the middle of it.

It is this kind of knowledge that has led a growing number of librarians to play a more active role in collaborative assignment design. All four of the librarians I interviewed engage in assignment design, and three noted their efforts to encourage other librarians to engage in such work.

Librarians' cross-disciplinary perspectives also played a significant role in collaboration. Because librarians work with students and instructors from a wide range of subject areas, they see how research and information use are approached through different disciplinary lenses. This often enables a fuller perspective on writing and research across the curriculum. Dan described this as an "umbrella view of the departments." Librarians, he reflected, interact with students who are studying different disciplines and are at different stages in their studies, and they see those students struggling with particular tasks and skills that are related to a program's larger, sequenced curriculum. This viewpoint can be especially useful when it comes to curricular planning with departments, since librarians pose questions and offer observations about where students struggle with particular tasks. This "umbrella" view has been beneficial for the WILD program, given its cross-curricular and disciplinary approach.

Such a cross-disciplinary perspective was also apparent in some librarians' knowledge of content areas outside of librarianship. Caroline, for example, reflected on her knowledge of and interest in instructional design, which strongly informs her library work and which she developed through self-directed learning and work with other campus instructional designers. As is the case for many librarians, Caroline's expertise extends beyond what is often associated with librarianship. A significant percentage of librarians enter the field after working in other professions, and many have subject expertise and advanced degrees in other disciplines. When Michelle began working with Caroline, she was impressed by Caroline's knowledge of composition and rhetoric, which contrasted with her own limited exposure to the literature on information literacy.

Michelle commented that composition and rhetoric appeared to exist in a kind of silo, while "it seems like by nature library work is interdisciplinary because if you're a librarian collaborating with a particular discipline you need to be at least somewhat familiar with the other literature." As Michelle explained, "I didn't have that same need in the other direction until I took on this role." In working with Caroline, Michelle has expanded her understanding of information literacy and her approach to teaching information literacy in her writing courses.

*Expanding Pedagogical Perspectives*

This experience of expanding one's own pedagogical perspectives was expressed by all of the interviewees. Largely because of the different ways that compositionists and librarians work with students, they often found that their own pedagogical approaches evolved through collaboration. Donna, who completed her library studies immediately after receiving her undergraduate degree, had a limited amount of teaching experience prior to her work with Teresa. She explained that she has become a more reflective teacher through their collaboration and her work is now more deeply informed by pedagogical theories and practice. Along with this has come a greater level of comfort with the messiness of teaching and learning. She related that her own and Teresa's pedagogical approaches are now very closely aligned.

At the same time, Teresa observed that through her work with Donna, she has become more sensitive and responsive to the "practical" and affective learning needs of students. While Teresa described herself as "so comfortable in chaos" and in the messy process of writing, working with Donna has helped her to recognize that her students may also sometimes need to experience more structure in their learning process. As Teresa explained, she now strives to offer students "some practical, material outcome for them to hang onto as they're floating through the [..] chaos, something to anchor them in the chaos." Teresa's comments suggest that, while it is important to recognize the messiness of writing and research, it is also valuable to provide students with varying degrees of structure and guidance as they work through various stages of their research. Writing teachers and librarians, in working together, may find more effective ways to balance the levels of structure and open-endedness they offer when asking students to engage in inquiry and source-based writing.

Donna and Teresa's comments reflect the ways that many partners found their pedagogical approaches becoming more aligned over the course of their interactions. They often came to recognize connections between information literacy and writing that had not been apparent to them before. Wendy, for example, commented that, "When we work with students it's all about the question now." This approach has been crucial for her and Stephanie as they challenge students' tendency "to create a thesis and then find sources the night before," as if sources could simply be inserted into a paper after all the analytical work was done. Relatedly, the two have begun to think differently about the role of thesis statements in first-year writing courses. Wendy observed that students are often asked in these courses to develop a thesis statement at the beginning of their research process, before they have had sufficient time to deepen their understanding of a topic. Wendy and Stephanie have therefore begun to ask questions like "What if at the end of the semester they don't have a thesis statement and they just keep it as a question? And [they] see their job not as trying to prove something but rather exploring an issue?" Such an approach, from their perspective, may help students to "go deeper than they [do] in a more traditional research paper." This argument for de-emphasizing thesis statements in first-year writing, I would add, does not mean that theses no longer have a place in writing courses; rather, the question might instead be where their place is and what instruction builds toward thesis development.

These kinds of pedagogical considerations, which are results of ongoing dialogue and collaboration, present new pedagogical possibilities. They also come with new challenges for teachers. Wendy observed that students do not always embrace teaching that creates more room for questioning and ambiguity. A more authentic and "messy" approach to question development is "sometimes painful for students and [...] for instructors." Wendy compared this to working in a writing center with students who simply wanted someone to correct their grammar. This difficulty is a reminder of the rich potential for writing-information literacy integrations that take an extended view of student learning. As Wendy asserted, "We're in it for the long game." While that approach "can be painful and slow," it also is the kind of strategy that is far more likely to foster the conceptual understandings and habits of mind that are key to deeper learning and "high-road" learning transfer, through which conceptual knowledge is applied to new situations.

Several librarian interviewees also noted shifts in how their library colleagues were thinking about librarians' instructional roles as extending beyond one-shot sessions to collaborative instructional planning with other educators. Stephanie described the increasing engagement among her library colleagues in principles of instructional design and in activities like collaborative assignment design. While this kind of work is new to many librarians, Stephanie has observed her colleagues expressing enthusiasm about these new directions for librarianship. Dan discussed the ACRL *Framework* as one catalyst for librarians to consider how teaching can encourage students to engage in a kind of "marinating" of ideas, as they consider what they wish to communicate about the information with which they engage. He contrasted this to the tendency in much of library instruction to think of information synthesis and use as things that occur outside of library instruction. A key part of this shift, Dan noted, is librarians' recognition that they have a valuable role to play in encouraging students to consider the contextual and rhetorical factors that ideally inform their research and writing processes. As this suggests, librarians' and compositionists' perceptions of their own professional and institutional roles have significant influence on the potential for meaningful partnerships. These self-perceptions are, of course, greatly influenced by the larger social and institutional contexts in which individuals work.

## *Institutional Positions*

Closely tied to individuals' perceptions of their professional roles were their institutional and departmental positions. Much like partners' complementary knowledge and experiences, their respective positions on campus also played powerful roles in these partnerships. Librarians—as "outsiders" to an academic department and who work across subject areas—could offer their interdisciplinary perspectives, as they posed questions about instruction or curricula that might not occur to those working every day in a given writing program. At the same time, librarians sometimes hesitated to raise issues during department or committee meetings that might be easier for a department member to introduce. Compositionists from that department could, as Michelle stated, often work as "translators" relaying sometimes similar messages in a different "voice" and language. For Michelle, this role of translator works well, largely because of her perspective on likely resistances in her program to information literacy instruction. Similarly, Teresa and Donna described Teresa as a campus "ambassador" for information literacy. Teresa's involvement as the Director of First-Year Writing on the Faculty Senate enables her to spark conversations about information literacy in both the First-Year Writing curriculum and in General Education development and assessment. The WILD program, which also involves both compositionists and librarians in broader curricular efforts, is another reminder of how library-writing program connections might further expand to include larger campus communities.

## Challenges to Growing Collaborative Community

At the same time that all interviewees expressed enthusiasm about the process and the results of their collaborations, they also reported significant challenges in gaining widespread engagement within their departments and campuses. The greatest difficulties related to three main themes:

- perceptions of information literacy as an "add-on," rather than as integral to a program's instructional goals;
- limited views of librarians' instructional roles and, relatedly, questions of professional territory; and
- limited time and resources

Closely tied to the first two themes are views among some compositionists and librarians (not those I interviewed) of library instruction as taking a somewhat limited shape (namely, that of introducing library search tools and basic search techniques). A conception of library instruction as separate from rhetorical and conceptual aspects of writing reflects an artificial separation that is often created between writing and research instruction, as was explored in Chapter 1. This view of writing and information literacy as existing in separate domains implies distinct lines between professional territories. While identifying differences between what writing instructors and librarians do in a given collaboration is important to negotiate, an over-emphasis on these distinctions can present obstacles to collaboration.

Perhaps the greatest challenge to expanding efforts beyond the limits of a single partnership was the perception of information literacy as an "add-on." Michelle, for example, commented that before her more intensive work with Caroline and her role as Information Literacy Coordinator for her writing program, information literacy was stated as a First-Year Writing course goal but was not always deeply integrated into composition curricula. At this point there had already been substantive conversations, workshops, and activities focused on information literacy, and information literacy was addressed through a collaboratively developed online tutorial that all first-year writing students completed. However, the depth of information literacy integration into a given course section depended on the motivation and interest of individual writing teachers. Some instructors stressed elements of information literacy throughout the research writing unit, while others relied on the tutorial, library seminar, and librarians to meet this course objective.

The lack of a teacher's engagement with these opportunities could be attributed to a number of possible factors that affect writing instructors, including fatigue with what might appear to be "add-ons"; competing demands and limited time; less experienced instructors feeling a sense of being overwhelmed; and the fact that there are over eighty first-year writing instructors (which naturally presents challenges to coordinating efforts). Michelle noted that during this time she had the view "That's [information literacy] what the library does." Although valuable conversations about information literacy were already occurring between Caroline and PWR leaders through curriculum committees, as well as through pre-semester training opportunities, the goal of integrating information literacy needed fuller support. Michelle's position as Information Literacy Coordinator was created in recognition of this need.

The perception of information literacy as something extra is not unique to the PWR program. Caroline and Michelle, sensitive to the fact that information literacy can be perceived as an initiative disconnected from central course goals, have sought to make clear that their approach to writing-information literacy integration "isn't an add-on." They seek to do this by "really examining and showing how it's [information literacy] already there [in what we teach in our writing and rhetoric classes] and then developing the language that helps writing faculty understand that." In other words, the goals and practices common to information literacy instruction align with those of writing and rhetoric pedagogy. This is especially evident in how compositionists and librarians encourage students to think critically, analytically, and rhetorically about the contextual nature of information.

Donna and Teresa have similarly struggled with limited conceptions of librarians' instructional roles that affect the potential for information literacy integration. As Teresa explained, many writing instructors in her program associate the library solely with assigning traditional research papers, a genre whose usefulness is being questioned in the field of composition. (This issue is explored further in Chapter 5.) The perception of information literacy as a separate entity also presents significant challenges to librarians who wish to extend their instructional role beyond a traditional one-shot library session. As Stephanie noted, "It's still really, really hard for librarians to get into classrooms and for librarians to build [instruction] tools that are used by anybody." Librarians, she reflected, "would still like to be seen as more of a collaborative partner," offering input on things like assignment design. Teaching roles for librarians' teaching are increasingly moving in this direction, but that change is gradual and must occur through thoughtful responses to resistances within both professions. The significant investment that went into integrating information literacy into the PWR program and the obstacles it faced with this effort shed light on the time, persistence, and patience that deep programmatic and curricular change involve.

The view of curricular initiatives as "add-ons" is, of course, not limited to information literacy and library instruction. Writing Across the Curriculum (WAC) and Writing in the Disciplines (WID) programs have struggled with similar misperceptions of their efforts.[9] While projects that bring together library and WAC/WID initiatives have been relatively limited, they clearly share common ground.[10] In the case of WILD, both compositionists and librarians are seeking to promote curricular change in courses for which neither are the actual course instructors. WID administrators generally take the leading role in this program, but the fact that neither the compositionists nor the librarians involved in this project are course instructors in the target programs creates a different dynamic between the compositionists and librarians involved. WILD is

---

9. Mike Rose, "The Language of Exclusion: Writing Instruction at the University," *College English* 47, no. 4 (1985): 341–59; Arno F. Knapper, "Good Writing--a Shared Responsibility," *Journal of Business Communication* 15, no. 2 (Winter 1978): 23–27; Martha Townsend, "WAC Program Vulnerability and What to Do About It," in *Writing Across the Curriculum : A Critical Sourcebook*, ed. Terry Myers Zawacki and Paul M. Rogers, Bedford/St. Martin's Series in Rhetoric and Compostition (Boston: Bedford/St. Martins, 2012), 543–56.

10. James K. Elmborg, "Information Literacy and Writing Across the Curriculum: Sharing the Vision," *Reference User Services Quarterly* 31, no. 1 (2003): 68–80; Jeanne Galvin, "Information Literacy and Integrative Learning," *College & Undergraduate Libraries* 13, no. 3 (2006): 25–51, doi:10.1300/J106v13n03-03; Jean Sheridan, ed., *Writing-Across-the-Curriculum and the Academic Library: A Guide for Librarians, Instructors, and Writing Program Directors* (Westport, CT: Greenwood Press, 1995).

therefore a particularly interesting example for considering possibilities for writing-library collaboration, as in this instance compositionists and librarians work collectively to challenge views of curricular initiatives as extrinsic from educators' own instructional priorities.

## Working toward Broader Curricular Change

In the WILD program at the University of Vermont, both compositionists and librarians are in a sense outsiders to an academic program, as they facilitate conversations and instructional planning with various departments. This position has both benefits and challenges. The challenges include the initial momentum required to bring together a group of faculty who balance many responsibilities and who may often feel overextended. Another difficulty is addressing perceptions of writing and of information literacy as separate skills that detract from a curriculum's content.

In light of this, one might think that simultaneously advocating for both writing and information literacy would present additional hurdles than would encouraging integration of only one of them. So it was to my surprise that Susanmarie commented during her conference presentation with Dan that WILD participants often perceived writing instruction as a more manageable task when paired with information literacy.[11] When I asked during our interview why this might be, Susanmarie described a common faculty perception of writing as something that cannot be taught but that is simply acquired without instruction. In contrast, many faculty appear to view information literacy as a more concrete and teachable skill. Writing and information literacy may seem more manageable when considered together, as instructors may see a focus on information literacy as providing a more structured approach upon which to build writing instruction. While conceptions of writing

---

11. Susanmarie Harrington, Dan De Santo, and Charlotte J. Mehrtens, "Getting WILD: Writing and Information Literacy in the Disciplines" (Georgia International Conference on Information Literacy, Savannah, Georgia, 2015), http://digitalcommons.georgiasouthern.edu/gaintlit/2015/2015/74/.

and information literacy as either amorphous and unteachable or as concrete and straightforward may not be accurate, in the WILD program these perceptions paradoxically may help to initiate dialogue across the disciplines about writing and information literacy instruction.

The grassroots, faculty-driven approach that characterizes WILD has also been an important quality of many Writing Across the Curriculum and Writing in the Disciplines programs. Such an approach, supported from the ground up, may be more likely to result in greater buy-in than do many institutional mandates. The WILD initiative has been possible primarily because of the joint engagement of the Writing in the Disciplines program, the library, and faculty across disciplines. As Susanmarie noted, "there is no incentive for doing this except that it's a great project." Engagement in WILD, in other words, must come out of a department's own belief in the value of the process. (Department liaisons also currently receive modest stipends for their efforts, whose amounts are equivalent to one course release. These funds come from a Davis Foundation grant, though the duration of that support is uncertain.) On the other hand, such grassroots efforts often receive limited funding, which can present challenges to sustaining a program. As Susanmarie noted, while many campus partners recognize the value of WILD, in the face of shifting budgets its lifespan is uncertain. The WILD program reflects the potential that exists for compositionists and librarians to combine efforts to support broader curricular change. At the same time, the uncertainty of its continued funding calls attention to the material challenges of such efforts and the need for widespread support within and across institutions.

The shared goals of many compositionists and librarians for broader curricular change were also a significant theme of my conversation with Teresa and Donna, who spoke in particular about the WPA and ACRL frameworks, which are reflective of both professions' efforts to contribute to national conversations about the purpose of higher education. Teresa expressed enthusiasm for what she saw as the greatest benefit of collaboration: to push back against efforts to standardize assessment and use quantitative measures that reduce student learning to numbers, and to instead encourage more holistic understandings of the messy and largely unquantifiable aspects of learning. Similarly, Donna reflected on the power of the frameworks for such broader efforts. For her, one of the great strengths of these documents is their openness to revision and their acknowledgement that "everything is always in flux." Reflecting specifically on the ACRL *Framework*, Donna asserted that "being able to acknowledge that everything is always in flux gives us a power…that we didn't have before because now we can bend and flex and align with the very similar work that colleagues in what I call our sister discipline [composition and rhetoric] are doing." Building on this idea and again thinking of higher education environments broadly, Donna described the potential for compositionists and librarians to work together and counter the push in higher education toward quantitative assessment and the over-emphasis on "measurable" outcomes. If our disciplinary scholarship and documents allow for a fuller view of student learning and a flexibility in how we approach instruction, she asserted, "we can flex together" in response to those trends.

These comments suggest the social and political significance of teaching writing and information literacy: that compositionists and librarians ideally help students develop their abilities to participate in discourse communities that might initially be less accessible, and that this participation is often essential to how students engage in the world and to what opportunities are accessible to them. As Teresa asserted, "working with information, working with writing–these are political acts," acts that "involve power." For her, it was important that professional documents like the frameworks address "the power that underlies working with information and working with students," particularly since "many people outside of our disciplines don't recognize those two aspects of the work that we do." Largely because writing and information literacy education play strong roles in whether or how students are able to engage in various communities and discourses, she finds it especially important for compositionists and librarians to join in their efforts.

## Professional and Institutional Status: A Cause for Solidarity or Distancing?

The political dimensions of teaching writing and information literacy are, of course, hardly limited to our interactions with students. They are also apparent in the relationships that compositionists and librarians develop with one another and in the positions we have within our respective institutions. If we are to cultivate deeper connections between writing programs and libraries, we must also look at these complex dynamics and how they function within institutional structures and hierarchies. The greatest obstacles to expanding partnerships are often inseparable from the larger institutional contexts and cultures in which compositionists and librarians find themselves.

One of the obstacles to dialogue and partnership may be rooted, ironically, in a shared experience of many compositionists and librarians: that of institutional marginalization. This is reflected in the peripheral role that writing and information literacy instruction often play in university curricula and, relatedly, in the lower status that the two professions have historically experienced within higher education. Though the issue of institutional status was not a focus of my interviews (this topic is explored in much greater depth in Chapter 5), it was a prominent theme of my conversation with Teresa and Donna. Their discussion illustrated that institutional social structures play a significant role in the potential for writing-library collaborations. Our discussions about these issues were particularly refreshing because up to that time I had only experienced librarians and compositionists talking about professional marginalization within their fields, not across them. As Teresa and Donna suggested, such conversations can be powerful openings not only for growing composition-library partnerships, but also for fostering broader institutional and curricular change. But given that such open dialogue also requires a considerable amount of trust, it is perhaps understandable that these kinds of discussions are not commonplace.

Throughout our conversation Teresa and Donna gave considerable attention to the challenges that institutional status and positioning often present to writing instructors and librarians. As we discussed, though a similar experience of marginalization might be a cause for solidarity, it may also function as a source of tension between the professions. When compositionists and librarians seek to illustrate the importance of writing and information literacy to other educators, individuals in each profession may often divert energy away from what the two professions might do collectively to support larger curricular change. Some might also hesitate to join efforts with others who experience a lower institutional status if they believe that such alignment could weaken rather than strengthen their own potential for effecting change.

When the theme of professional marginalization emerged during our conversation, I asked Teresa and Donna if they had ideas about why there is not more solidarity between the two professions, given their similar goals and challenges. Teresa believed that a lack of awareness in composition about information literacy and the instructional work of librarians could explain part of this separation. She reflected on her lack of knowledge about these topics when she and Donna first began working together, but she also believed that institutional status plays a significant role. The fact that Donna has faculty status on her campus (something which is not true for all academic librarians) may have made it easier for the two to work together, particularly since their work could be justified by connecting it to a research agenda that is required for receiving tenure. As this implies, the differences in perceived status of the two professions might be greater on other campuses. Teresa also reflected on the material conditions of working in a university and the fact that individuals are often vying for resources. This is likely to discourage collaboration, particularly with others who might not possess a higher social standing. In light of this environment, Teresa noted that individuals already working in a marginalized field may be less inclined to align themselves with another marginalized field on campus if they were concerned that doing so could further limit their own agency.

The experience of existing on the periphery may also be understood in relation to the process-oriented and context-dependent nature of writing and information literacy. As Donna indicated, the lack of recognition that writing and information literacy instruction often receive may be explained largely by the fact that "these processes, when they're done well, are invisible." Nonetheless, Donna observed, composition has a clear place in the curriculum that information literacy does not, at least on their campus where there is no credit-bearing information literacy course. At the same time, teaching for-credit courses clearly does not remove all hierarchical barriers. Teresa saw the lower status of composition and of librarianship as due, in part, to "a difference in ethos of the scholarship of teaching and learning and scholarship in the disciplines." The former, which is often the focus of composition-ists and instruction librarians, tends to be viewed as less rigorous and serious than the latter.

Teresa and Donna's collaboration, like the other partnerships discussed in this chapter, nonetheless illustrates that even though these concerns are often real and legitimate, compositionists and librarians have far more to gain by joining in their efforts. In so doing, we are better positioned to challenge limited conceptions of writing and information literacy that do not benefit our professions or our students. These kinds of deeper collaborations will ideally involve compositionists and librarians examining their conceptions of information literacy instruction, as well as the ways in which each profession conceives of and interacts with the other. In the next chapter I explore such issues more deeply by considering the similar historical origins and developments of composition and library instruction, as well as sociological perspectives on librarian-faculty relations.

## Emerging Themes and Their Implications

As the collaborations explored in this chapter illustrate, the benefits and challenges that librarians and compositionists experience in building partnerships are greatly influenced by a range of factors and circumstances. Just as writing and information literacy are highly contextual activities, so too are collaborations. While no two partnerships are identical, several prominent themes emerged throughout these conversations. Among the key factors that drive meaningful collaboration are:

- the importance of shared goals, mutual appreciation of one another's unique expertise and experience, and ongoing dialogue to enable successful collaboration;
- the influence that cross-professional collaboration can have on practitioners' evolving pedagogical approaches;
- recognition of and appreciation for the converging pedagogical approaches among compositionists and librarians, similarities that have become increasingly more apparent since the adoption of the ACRL *Framework*;
- the potential to support broader curricular change that foregrounds students as lifelong learners and that challenges the push in education toward standardized and quantitative assessment of student learning; and
- the value of expanding cross-professional dialogue about larger structural factors that affect composition and information literacy education and compositionists' and librarians' involvement in those efforts.

Interviewees' successes appeared to have been largely possible because individuals shared an understood goal as well as pedagogical perspectives which aligned with that goal. They engaged in ongoing dialogue and appreciated one another's unique contributions to achieving that goal, while they also seemed to enjoy the process itself. People conveyed enthusiasm and excitement when describing projects and conversations to which they brought their creative energies.

At the same time that these benefits seem clear, interviewees experienced notable challenges with expanding collaboration to other writing instructors, librarians, and academic programs. Common difficulties included time constraints, institutional support, and perhaps most importantly, the challenge of conveying the relevance and value of collaboration to colleagues. Such challenges make clear that the growth of such initiatives ultimately requires that compositionists and librarians respond to their programs' and institutions' cultures and material realities. The work toward fuller integration of information literacy and writing integration, as with writing and information literacy development, is a long-term and gradual process, in which the greatest gains are likely to come from continued dialogue and engagement. The investment that such work entails may help to explain why collaboration between compositionists and librarians has not been greater. These common obstacles illustrate the need for stronger institutional supports and cultures of collaboration that foster student-centered curricular change.

To grow these partnerships also requires that we examine the barriers to collaboration that are rooted in the larger sociocultural and structural conditions that affect our professional roles and everyday work. In the following chapter I continue to consider the possibilities for and challenges to collaboration while focusing on the historical, sociocultural, and institutional conditions that powerfully influence our pedagogical work and our institutional positions. An awareness of commonalities and distinctions betweenthe experiences of compositionists and librarians in relation to these contexts can better provide both professions with deeper understandings of one another's work and thus can better enable us to recognize and respond to barriers to collaboration.

# Chapter 5

## Expanding the Potential for Collaborations: Intersections between the Interpersonal and the Sociostructural

Collaborations like those described in Chapter 4 illustrate the shared goals and interests of compositionists and librarians, as well as the possibilities that exist when we combine our instructional efforts. These partnerships also convey the importance of building relationships, being sensitive to local contexts, and recognizing shared goals when expanding cross-professional ties. Parallel histories and similar professional challenges for compositionists and librarians (a focal point of this chapter) may help in identifying shared goals that can be a basis for collaboration.

The limited dialogue about pedagogy between compositionists and librarians may have more to do with professional cultures and institutional structures than we sometimes realize or openly acknowledge. In my experiences as a librarian, many of my library colleagues recognize and are eager to talk within the profession about interpersonal dynamics and structural conditions that prevent meaningful partnerships with other educators, but it is less common for such discussions to extend beyond our profession. During such conversations it can easily feel as if librarians are alone in their particular frustrations, when in reality others, including compositionists, may be grappling with similar, albeit not necessarily identical, issues.

Though initial conversations between writing instructors and librarians about shared interests are unlikely to begin by looking at structural barriers (and though we may be wise to consider carefully when and how we approach such topics), this chapter works from the idea that building meaningful librarian-faculty partnerships will ultimately be more successful when librarians and compositionists consider not only instructional scenarios in which collaboration makes sense, but also the cultures and systems in which we work and how those environments may foster or limit the potential for open discussion and collaboration. Of course, these structural conditions are often the most difficult issues to address. While it may prove more effective at many institutions to approach such topics after a collaborative relationship has already been well established, I believe that individuals in both professions need to seek more opportunities for constructively discussing structural and institutional barriers to collaboration and possible responses to them. Though many such conversations may begin within our individual fields, they also need to converge more frequently than they currently do.

With this perspective, I shift the focus in this chapter to sociocultural and structural factors that affect the everyday work and professional interactions of compositionists and librarians, conditions that often stand in the way of dialogue and collaboration. These circumstances can be better understood in light of the shared origins and unique developments of composition and of library instruction. Awareness of these histories helps to contextualize similar and differing challenges that compositionists and librarians have experienced in achieving institutional recognition, particularly as our work has become professionalized within academia. Though compositionists' and librarians' institutional positions are clearly distinct, the historical developments of writing and library instruction reflect how each is inevitably affected by and responsive to the hierarchical structures of academia and the power relations that come with them. By strengthening our conscious awareness of how these issues relate to our professional histories and institutional positions, compositionists and librarians can deepen the potential for working as equal partners toward shared pedagogical goals.

I begin this chapter by considering writing and library instruction's shared roots in literacy education. This historical context sheds light on how the perception of literacy education as remedial has contributed to the sometimes peripheral place of writing and information literacy instruction in college curricula, as well as to the institutional status and positioning of compositionists and librarians. After briefly discussing historical origins that have influenced writing and information literacy's curricular positions, I move my focus to scholarship on librarian-faculty relations. I admittedly give greater attention here to librarians' experiences of their instructional and institutional roles than to those of compositionists. This is partly because, as a librarian, I have much greater knowledge and experience with this topic, while I do not feel as well positioned to express the perspectives and experiences of writing instructors. But this emphasis can also be explained by the reality that librarians' teaching is most often done in support of another instructor's course and is thus inevitably collaborative. The opportunities and the challenges that result from this dynamic are reflected in a notable amount of academic literature on librarian-faculty relations. Such scholarship often indicates that librarians generally have a lesser degree of influence over what occurs in college classrooms and curricula.

This general discussion of librarian-faculty relations leads into a more particular consideration of disjunctures that often exist between the library and writing classrooms. Finally, I argue for reexamining and reframing our individual and shared work in mutually supportive ways that help to grow pedagogical approaches to "writing information literacy." Then, in the subsequent and final chapter, I consider further how librarians and compositionists who share common pedagogical goals might help to strengthen composition-library partnerships, in large part through awareness of and productive responses to the sociocultural and structural environments that influence our everyday work and relationships.

## Parallel Histories and Shared Experiences

Composition and information literacy instruction's shared roots in literacy education, in addition to the parallels between their unique historical developments, reflect both common and distinct experiences of compositionists and librarians. James Elmborg (a library science professor who has worked as both a writing instructor and a librarian) discusses these connections in his 2003 article, "Information Literacy and Writing Across the Curriculum: Sharing the Vision."[1] Writing to academic librarians, Elmborg illustrates how the Writing Across the Curriculum (WAC) movement–and composition studies more generally–can offer insight into the circumstances of and possibilities for information literacy education:

> Because of the many similarities in their missions and visions these two general education initiatives share a set of problems and questions that have recurred over the past 100 years, almost the entire history of the curriculum, as we know it.[2]

As Elmborg argues, these issues revolve around a larger struggle of both compositionists and librarians to locate an "appropriate place in the college curriculum" for writing and information literacy, respectively, a struggle that is bound up in issues of institutional structure and power.[3] Elmborg identifies three lines of questioning related to this difficulty:

- questions of responsibility (i.e., Who teaches writing and research?)
- questions of remediation (i.e., Should institutions of higher education be responsible for teaching "basic skills" that students

---

1. James K. Elmborg, "Information Literacy and Writing Across the Curriculum: Sharing the Vision," *Reference User Services Quarterly* 31, no. 1 (2003): 68–80. Writing across the curriculum, or WAC, programs gained considerable momentum in the 1980s and 1990s and continue to influence teaching at many colleges and universities today. WAC works from the idea that writing is best developed when integrated within and across subject areas and emphasize the act of writing as highly contextual and writing instruction as a shared responsibility of all educators. Efforts toward curricular integration of information literacy share a very similar goal and premise.

2. James Elmborg, "Critical Information Literacy: Implications for Instructional Practice," *Journal of Academic Librarianship* 32, no. 2 (2006): 68.

3. Elmborg, "Information Literacy and Writing Across the Curriculum,." 68.

are often expected to already possess when entering college? What are the consequences of viewing writing and information literacy as remedial?)

- questions of accountability (i.e., Who should be held responsible for whether or not students are able to write and to research when they come to college?)

According to Elmborg, "[t]hese questions set the grounds for the debate regarding both library instruction and composition instruction for the first three-quarters of the twentieth century and they remain pertinent in discussions today."[4] Their relevance to librarians now, thirteen years after Elmborg wrote his piece, has perhaps become even greater, as librarians have become more intensely engaged in reexamining their pedagogies and, along with them, their institutional roles.

## Perceptions of Literacy Education and the Implications for Curricular Change

The lines of questioning that Elmborg relates to writing and information literacy are reminders of a common perception that literacy is a procedural and easily acquired skill. Such an understanding of literacy—and by extension of writing and information literacy—is rooted in a longer history of literacy education, which in its earlier days centered primarily on teaching the "correct" use of English. The rhetoric surrounding literacy education in the United States has repeatedly implied that such instruction is remedial and corrective, a necessary skill that prepares students for the more rigorous and "real" work of college.

It is worth noting, as many literacy studies scholars and compositionists have pointed out, that such a view of literacy problematically implies that discursive practices should be uniform, or that communication that does not conform to Standard English is inferior and incorrect, rather

---

4. Ibid. 68.

than a meaningful reflection and expression of a particular culture or community. The fields of literacy studies and of composition and rhetoric have done a great deal of work to challenge such reductionist views of language and literacy, as many scholars in these areas have instead stressed the diversity of literacy practices and their socially and culturally situated nature. However, literacy education generally and writing and information literacy instruction more specifically are still influenced by the view that academic discourse is superior, rather than one discursive mode among many. The privileged status of academic discourse can also be understood in relation to a longer history of literacy education. For example, some literacy scholars have made a convincing argument that literacy education has functioned throughout history largely as a means of reinforcing a dominant culture and discourse and of devaluing other linguistic and discursive practices, particularly those of ethnic minorities and immigrants.

Writing instruction, in its early emphasis on proper grammar and syntax, played a significant role in maintaining a certain social structure and cultural values in this climate. As James Berlin writes in *Writing Instruction in Nineteenth-Century American Colleges*, writing instructors became "caretakers of the English tongue" and the "gatekeepers on the road to the good things in life."[5] Writing instruction's early focus on grammatical correctness, Berlin explains, "gave support to the view that has haunted writing classes ever since: learning to write is learning matters of superficial correctness."[6] In this environment, English composition textbooks treated Standard English as *the* English, while ignoring the reality that the English language in the United States was in many respects changing along with the ethnic diversification of the United States. As David R. Russell explains, "Standards of literacy were no longer stable; they were rising, and more importantly, multiplying."[7]

---

5. James A. Berlin, *Writing Instruction in Nineteenth-Century American Colleges*, Studies in Writing & Rhetoric (Carbondale: Southern Illinois University Press, 1984), 72–73.

6. Ibid., 62.

7. David R. Russell, *Writing in the Academic Disciplines: A Curricular History*, 2nd ed. (Carbondale: Southern Illinois University Press, 2002), 6.

The role of writing instruction in maintaining the notion of a proper universal form of English that sustains a certain social structure is not limited to the late nineteenth century. This is especially evident in literacy crises and campaigns of the 1960s and 1970s when, with the implementation of open admissions policies in college enrollment, student bodies again became more diverse. This time it was the GI Bill that largely contributed to this dramatic increase and diversification of college students. It is also around this time that new "literacy crises" emerged. Popular articles like Merrill Sheils' *Newsweek* piece "Why Johnny Can't Write" alarmed Americans about declining rates of functional literacy among its youth, with "statistics that grow more appalling each year."[8] Although such literacy crises have been more directly associated with writing programs that were intended to initiate students into more formal, academic, and "appropriate" ways of writing and speaking, library instruction in many respects shares this history of literacy education. Learning how to do academic research and how to use scholarly sources is similarly a means of initiation into the scholarly discourse from which many, if not most, students feel alienated.

The view of literacy as operating in a singular, correct mode fits with that of writing and information literacy as mechanical skills. Writing Across the Curriculum and Writing in the Disciplines programs have made significant progress in challenging such views of composition, and many library instruction programs and initiatives are accomplishing similar goals for information literacy education. However, misperceptions about writing and information literacy are still not uncommon among students, college educators, and administrators. This impacts how compositionists' and librarians' teaching and instructional programs are valued, structured, and implemented.

The fact that literacy education has often been perceived of as remedial suggests yet another essential connection between compositionists' and instruction librarians' professions: our institutional positioning. Both compositionists and instruction librarians have often experienced

---

8. Merrill Sheils, "Why Johnny Can't Write," *Newsweek* 92, no. 8 (1975): 58.

peripheral roles in their institutions, largely because teaching "basic" skills is often perceived in colleges and universities as less intellectually rigorous and prestigious than work in other academic fields. Our social and political positioning at local institutions and within the larger context of higher education, in combination with views of writing and information literacy instruction as corrective, inevitably affect the potential for integrating writing and information literacy at the curricular level, a process that many in our professions agree is essential for supporting student learning. Although compositionists and librarians are often viewed as those responsible for teaching writing and information literacy respectively, professionals in our fields are well aware that what we teach cannot be mastered through a single course; nor should that pedagogy be reduced to "basic" skills that transfer perfectly from one situation or one discipline to the next.

## Parallel but Distinct Histories

Both compositionists and librarians have resisted reductionist conceptions of literacy and of their instructional work as our fields have become professionalized. Academic training and the development of research and scholarship has helped to establish writing and information literacy as areas of study. Such work has enriched pedagogical approaches to both writing and information literacy education. The timelines on which these changes have occurred in each field are distinct, as are the circumstances that shape teaching in each profession. While the shared origins of writing and information literacy instruction can help inform compositionists' and librarians' teaching, so too can differences in the developments and current conditions affecting writing and library instruction. These distinctions include professional, institutional, and structural contexts that influence writing and information literacy programs.

By and large, writing programs have become more widely established and institutionally supported in higher education than library instruction initiatives. As Elmborg explains, composition programs, in contrast to library instruction programs and services, have been housed within English departments that confer academic degrees and that employ full-time faculty whose work is dedicated primarily to teaching. This structure greatly facilitated the professionalization of writing studies, a process that became especially evident in the 1980s, as English departments established doctoral programs in composition and rhetoric.[9] As these doctoral programs grew, English compositionists began to develop pedagogical approaches and research agendas informed by educational theories and work in disciplines such as educational psychology, linguistics, literary studies, and cultural studies. Composition studies also had a more grounded footing when it came to teaching undergraduate curricula. This further enabled writing programs to initiate and support cross-disciplinary approaches to writing instruction, which have been the focal point of the Writing Across the Curriculum movement.

Librarians, in contrast, did not benefit from the advantages of working in an academic department that offers degrees and that usually teaches credit-bearing courses.[10] The growth of credit-bearing information literacy courses taught by librarians is a more recent and still relatively uncommon phenomenon. Moreover, librarians have long been viewed as helpful people whose responsibilities revolve primarily around providing access to information resources. Instruction and scholarship have generally been seen as absent or ancillary to librarianship (though this is no longer the reality for a large and growing percentage of academic librarians). Nonetheless, librarian-led instruction still is most often far more limited in scope and by time constraints than are most writing classes.[11] The amount of contact librarians have with students highlights

---

9. Elmborg, "Information Literacy and Writing Across the Curriculum," 69.

10. Ibid., 68.

11. As noted earlier, although approaches to information literacy education are shifting, most library instruction still occurs as one or two stand-alone sessions for a credit-bearing course taught by an instructor other than the librarian. Within this model, librarians often take the role of a guest lecturer who briefly introduces aspects of a research process that is far more complex than is suggested by the structure and time constraints of a one-shot library instruction session.

the significant challenges librarians generally have with gaining institutional traction and influencing educational reform.

In this context, it is unsurprising that the field of English composition has explored its theoretical underpinnings and developed related pedagogical and curricular models more fully than have most library instruction programs. At the same time, an increased interest in educational theory among librarians is reflected in a rapidly growing body of professional literature on information literacy. The growth of theoretical discussions about library instruction becomes increasingly evident in literature from the late 1980s and early 1990s, the time when the term "information literacy" begins to be closely associated with library instruction. Such work has become more prevalent as librarians' roles have become progressively more specialized (with some librarian positions focusing exclusively on teaching and learning) and as instruction has become an increasingly significant part of many librarians' jobs. Much of this scholarship and research comes from fields that also inform composition and rhetoric, such as educational psychology, literacy studies, and critical theory.

Along with an increasing interest among librarians in educational theories and in the connections between theory and practice, approaches to information literacy education have also expanded beyond one-shot sessions to initiatives meant to better integrate information literacy into and across courses. Such efforts include credit-bearing information literacy courses, collaborative assignment and course design, faculty workshops on teaching research, co-taught courses, and online learning objects such as tutorials and course-specific research guides. These changes in information literacy pedagogy often require that librarians reconsider their instructional roles and relationships to other educators, particularly as they advocate for the integration of information literacy into the curriculum. While most librarians would agree that the profession is in the very early stages of such work, these efforts appear to be increasing substantially. Such changes also suggest a growing convergence between the views of many librarians and compositionists toward teaching and learning.

The different timelines with which librarians and compositionists have deepened their engagement with pedagogical theories and research may help to explain why fuller collaborations between the two professions have been slow to develop. Though many librarians have challenged mechanical definitions of information literacy for decades, and though the concept of "information literacy" promoted by the Association of College and Research Libraries (ACRL) has from its beginnings been linked to critical thinking, the prevalence of theoretically-informed library instruction was fairly limited until recently. It is unsurprising that most college teachers, including most compositionists, are still unaware of the expanding contributions that librarians can and are making to teaching outside of the traditional databases demonstration.

The lack of awareness of what librarians do and have to offer to larger instructional efforts is being addressed partly through library outreach and new ways of structuring and offering library instructional services. But the challenge of shifting perceptions of librarians' teaching roles is, of course, much more complex than expanding communication. Particularly since librarians' teaching tends to depend largely on collaboration with other instructors, this work must also be understood in relation to the larger educational environments in which librarians work and interact with students and other educators.

Beyond the challenges for both librarians and compositionists of expanding teaching partnerships and supporting larger curricular efforts are larger questions about why so many educators do not recognize the complexity of what librarians and compositionists teach. Perhaps even more puzzling is the common disconnect between the work that librarians and compositionists do, despite rich common ground. As touched upon at the end of Chapter 4, the same challenges that our professions have faced with status and the misperceptions of our work may contribute to this disconnect.

## Institutional Culture, Professional Status, and Challenges to Curricular Change

Librarians and compositionists' curricular efforts further illustrate that our professions share common experiences that can serve as foundations for dialogue and collaboration. Many in both fields express a concern that academic cultures often do not prioritize instruction and resist collaboration. Many in our professions are particularly aware of these issues because they have experienced challenges with initiating and sustaining curricular efforts intended to engage faculty across disciplines.

As discussed earlier, the difficulties of such curricular work are due partly to limited understandings of what compositionists and librarians teach. A notable amount of literature from librarianship and from composition addresses these challenges from a sociological perspective. For example, in his 1995 article "Faculty Culture and Bibliographic Instruction: An Exploratory Analysis," librarian Larry Hardesty looked to sociological research to make better sense of librarians' difficulties with increasing collaboration with traditional teaching faculty. Though there have been significant changes in library instructional services since the time of Hardesty's writing, the key issues he identifies are still relevant and likely to resonate with writing instructors engaged in campus-wide curricular efforts. Informed by sociological research on faculty culture, Hardesty argues that many of their qualities and common values stand in the way of collaboration. These include "a feeling of lack of time; emphasis on content, professional autonomy, and academic freedom; de-emphasis on the applied and the process of learning; and resistance to change."[12] Often when faculty hold these values, Hardesty argues,

---

12. Larry Hardesty, "Faculty Culture and Bibliographic Instruction: An Exploratory Analysis," *Library Trends* 44, no. 2 (1995): 356; David R. Russell, "The Writing-Across-the-Curriculum Movement: 1970-1990," in *Writing Across the Curriculum: A Critical Sourcebook*, edited by Terry Myers Zawacki and Paul M. Rogers, Bedford/St. Martin's Series in Rhetoric and Compostition (Boston: Bedford/St. Martins, 2012), 31.

they "are not interested in 'bright ideas' from librarians about bibliographic instruction.[13]

Many compositionists involved in curricular initiatives to expand the role of writing instruction across the disciplines will be familiar with this frustration. David Russell describes similar characteristics of faculty culture that present obstacles to Writing Across the Curriculum (WAC) initiatives: "Faculty are naturally hesitant to risk a reexamination of their roles as teachers and as representatives of a discipline. Thus, relatively few faculty commit themselves to WAC."[14] From Russell's perspective, this tendency has a great deal to do with institutional values and reward structures that tend to prioritize disciplinary research over teaching:

> Even faculty who recognize the importance of writing for improving learning may not have the time to restructure their courses in ways that further integrate writing, for faculty must work within institutional and disciplinary contexts that embody competing values. The century-old complaint of faculty that they do not have time to assign and to respond to student writing is frequently a just one, but it begs larger questions of institutional values. What is less common in higher education is a substantial change in the way teaching is assessed and rewarded in the institution.[15]

This implies a need to look beyond our individual interactions with other educators to the larger systems in which teachers across our institutions work. Russell argues that these larger institutional values and structures, mirrored in things like tenure and promotion criteria and merit pay, must be reexamined if WAC is "to become more than a marginal activity."[16] As he asserts,

> If writing is to become a central focus of pedagogy, then it must be structurally linked to the values, goals, and activities of disciplines; faculty

---

13. Hardesty, "Faculty Culture and Bibliographic Instruction," 356.

14. Russell, "The Writing-Across-the-Curriculum Movement: 1970-1990," 31.

15. Ibid., 32.

16. Ibid.

must see a connection between encouraging better writing among their students and advancing the value and status of the disciplines —and of their own individual careers. Disciplines must find or create places where student writing matters to the disciplinary community.[17]

This same argument can be made for other curricular initiatives, including those centered on information literacy.

The peripheral role that writing and information literacy have generally played in college curricula is further evident in compositionists' and librarians' experiences of professional marginalization. Mike Rose has been among those to draw attention to the challenges compositions have faced in having their work recognized within the academy. In his 1985 essay "The Language of Exclusion: Writing Instruction at the University," Rose articulated such frustrations:

> [T]hough writing courses are highly valued and even enjoying a boom, they are also viewed with curious eyes. Administrators fund them—often generously—but academic senates worry that the boundaries between high school and college are eroding, and worry as well that the considerable investment of resources in such courses will drain money from the research enterprise. They deny some of the courses curricular status by tagging them remedial, and their members secretly or not-so-secretly wish the courses could be moved to community colleges.[18]

Even within the English departments that house writing programs there has often been a lack of appreciation for such courses, which are frequently taught by part-time instructors and graduate students who do not receive the same privileges or status as tenured and tenure-track faculty. Rose continues,

> English departments hold onto writing courses but consider the work intellectually second-class. The people who teach writing are more often than not temporary hires; their courses are robbed of curricular

---

17. Ibid., 37.

18. Mike Rose, "The Language of Exclusion: Writing Instruction at the University," *College English* 47, no. 4 (1985): 342.

continuity and of the status that comes with tenured faculty involvement. And the instructors? Well, they're just robbed.[19]

Rose draws connections here between perceptions of and attitudes about writing courses, the challenges of teaching general writing courses that often seem isolated from a broader curriculum, and the unjust working conditions of so many writing instructors, many of whom have contingent positions.

The field of composition and rhetoric has certainly become more firmly established and respected in academia since Rose wrote his article in 1985, but much of what he described still applies to writing programs. This is especially evident in the rise of contingent faculty in higher education, which affects writing programs disproportionately. The growing numbers of adjunct faculty who teach writing courses and the poor working conditions that accompany contingent positions are perhaps the most obvious indicators of the low regard commonly given to writing courses and programs. Despite the fact that the field has become more widely recognized as an area worthy of scholarly study since Rose's essay, the trend of hiring contingent and part-time faculty has worsened substantially in recent years.[20]

The influence of institutional values on the labor structure of writing programs can also be understood to some extent in gendered terms. As noted by Eileen Schell, a disproportionate percentage of contingent positions in college writing programs are held by women. Similarly to Rose, Schell argues that compositionists need to make efforts to address the larger systems that affect that nature of writing programs (in this case, "the gendered politics of contingent labor"), which she identifies as "one of the most pressing political problems in composition studies."[21]

---

19. Ibid.

20. For more recent statistics on contingent labor in higher education see: The Coalition on the Academic Workforce, "A Portrait of Part-Time Faculty Members," June 2012, http://www.academicworkforce.org/CAW_portrait_2012.pdf.

21. Eileen E. Schell, *Gypsy Academics and Mother-Teachers: Gender, Contingent Labor, and Writing Instruction, Crosscurrents* (Portsmouth, NH: Boynton/Cook Publishers, 1998), 4.

It is worth noting here that both English composition and librarianship are predominantly female professions and that issues of gender likely affect the social status of both professions.

Librarianship has fortunately not been as dramatically affected by the increased use of contingent faculty (though it also has not been untouched by it). The lower rank that most librarians experience is evident to some extent in the differing ranks and classification across academic institutions for librarian positions, which range from staff to professional academic to non-tenure track and tenure-track faculty. But this lower status is perhaps most apparent in interpersonal relationships with teaching faculty, in which power relations often play a role. These dynamics have been a topic of concern to academic librarians for decades, and their significance to the profession has become increasingly apparent as a growing number of librarians have sought to shift their pedagogical approaches and, along with them, their instructional roles.

Discussions about librarians' instructional and institutional roles often intersect with concerns about the traditional service model of librarianship, in which librarians have generally experienced limited autonomy in their teaching. This service model has been a strong characteristic of the field since its early days and is apparent in the nature of most library instruction. As noted earlier, library instruction is usually done in support of a credit-bearing class taught by another instructor and therefore depends largely on the engagement of other teachers. This is reflected in a significant amount of library literature on the importance and difficulty of collaborating with teaching faculty. Much of this work calls attention the unequal status and power of librarians in relation to teaching faculty. As Hardesty observes, "Part of the problem of the acceptance of bibliographic instruction is that it comes from a group that many faculty do not view as peers– librarians."[22] He substantiates this claim with literature written by both librarians and faculty. Articles like "Librarians as Teachers: The Study of an Organizational Fiction" (1979) reflect an early resistance on the part of some faculty to librarians

---

22. Hardesty, "Faculty Culture and Bibliographic Instruction," 356.

having any place in the classroom.[23] Similarly, Patricia Knapp, who in the 1960s sought to bring together librarians and faculty to integrate information literacy into Monteith College's curriculum, found that faculty did not fully accept librarians as members of the faculty and that some faculty did not accept them as peers.[24] Some teaching faculty have also observed this tendency to hold librarians at a distance. Earlham College English professor Gordon W. Thompson states in his 1993 essay that "faculty members regard librarians as they regard secretaries and ground keepers, as their errand boys and girls, not as their colleagues."[25] Hardesty also references a number of faculty surveys conducted by librarians in the 1980s which indicated that many faculty do not allow librarians into their professional circles.[26] I will return to this idea of library instruction as a service again shortly, as I look more closely at professional literature on librarian-faculty relations.

The literature from composition studies and from academic librarianship reviewed here helps contextualize the shared concerns of both fields that Elmborg articulated in his 2003 article "Information Literacy and Writing Across the Curriculum: Sharing the Vision." These again include:

- questions of responsibility (i.e., Who teaches writing and research?)
- questions of remediation (i.e., Should institutions of higher education be responsible for teaching "basic skills" that students are often expected to already possess when entering college?

---

23. Pauline Wilson, "Librarians as Teachers: The Study of an Organization Fiction," *Library Quarterly* 49, no. 2 (1979): 146–62.

24. Patricia B. Knapp, *The Monteith College Library Experiment* (New York: Scarecrow Press, 1966).

25. Gordon W. Thompson, "Faculty Recalcitrance about Bibliographic Instruction," in *Bibliographic Instruction in Practice: A Tribute to the Legacy of Evan Farber*, ed. Larry L. Hardesty, Jamie Hastreiter, and David Henderson, Library Orientation Series 24 (Ann Arbor, MI: Pierian Press, 1993), 103.

26. Hardesty, "Faculty Culture and Bibliographic Instruction," 357.

What are the consequences of viewing writing and information literacy in this way?)

- questions of accountability (i.e., Who should be held responsible for whether or not students are able to write and research when they come to college?)[27]

Because most librarians' teaching depends so heavily on collaboration with disciplinary faculty, library-faculty relations is a topic that deserves closer attention.

## Librarian-Faculty Relations

The fact that librarianship usually takes a form distinct from that of traditional teaching faculty positions (while composition studies fits into this model much more easily) contributes to unique challenges for librarians in building meaningful teaching partnerships. Given the unique nature of librarians' institutional positions and roles on their campuses, it is unsurprising that their relationships with disciplinary faculty are complex. The fact that many teaching faculty do not perceive of librarians as peers can be partly explained by very real structural and material reasons. As noted earlier, librarians usually do not usually teach credit courses and have a different range of job responsibilities. Moreover, the standard educational training for librarianship is less extensive and more practical than theoretical, which may further contribute to a sense of division between what librarians and other college educators do. All of these factors may be understood in relation to hierarchical structures in academia, which generally do not privilege work that is considered more practical and service-oriented.

In my review of the literature of library-faculty relations that is described in this chapter, I identified three prominent and interrelated themes that may help in better understanding faculty-librarian dynamics and how they affect the potential for meaningful teaching partnerships:

---

27. Elmborg, "Information Literacy and Writing Across the Curriculum," 68.

- the prevalence of an asymmetrical relationship between librarians and disciplinary faculty, in which faculty are perceived as having more status and authority;
- common misconceptions among disciplinary faculty of information literacy and of librarians' instructional roles as centered on the procedural; and
- the traditional service model and culture of librarianship that often reflects and reinforces librarians' lower status.

These themes reflect significant obstacles to building successful teaching partnerships. They stand in contrast to what Ruth Ivey has identified as key characteristics of successful librarian-faculty partnerships. As noted in Chapter 4, Ivey found through interviews with librarians and disciplinary faculty that successful partnerships were characterized by the following characteristics: a shared and understood goal; mutual respect, tolerance, and trust; competence for the task at hand; and engagement in ongoing dialogue.[28] These same themes were prominent in my interviews with the compositionist-librarian partners whose work is described in Chapter 4. Open dialogue, along with qualities like mutual respect and trust, is less likely to develop when a significant power imbalance is in place. Part of the goal of this chapter is to examine such dynamics and to consider more generative ways that librarians and other educators, including compositionists, can engage with one another.

## Asymmetrical Relationships

Interactions between librarians and disciplinary faculty can often be characterized by asymmetrical levels of investment, engagement, and power, as Lars Christiansen, Mindy Strombler, and Lyn Thaxton found in a sociological analysis of the library literature on faculty-librarian

---

28. Ruth Ivey, "Information Literacy: How Do Librarians and Academics Work in Partnership to Deliver Effective Learning Programs?", *Australian Academic & Research Libraries* 34, no. 2 (June 2003): 102.

relations. This "asymmetrical disconnection," the authors explain, can be characterized by librarians' comparatively fuller understanding of teaching faculty's work and greater interest in collaboration, by teaching faculty's higher social status, and by the fact that only librarians appeared to see the asymmetry as problematic. Key factors of the asymmetry between librarians and disciplinary faculty that emerged from this literature review included:

- asymmetrical understandings of one another's work (Librarians appeared to have a fuller knowledge of and interest in what faculty's work involved than did faculty in librarians' work.)
- a contrast between a library culture of sharing and collaboration and a disciplinary faculty culture that emphasized autonomy and independent work
- organizational factors such as differing responsibilities and separate work spaces, which limit opportunities for face-to-face interaction (particularly given the growing use of online resources that make visits to physical library spaces less necessary)
- differing social statuses, which were reflected in perceptions of librarian work as service-oriented and faculty work as focused on the production and dissemination of knowledge (Sociological research indicates the former to be less valued in our society. This likely contributes to status differences between these groups.)[29]

This imbalance clearly presents challenges to collaboration. It also helps to explain the common misconception among teaching faculty that information literacy is primarily procedural, since many disciplinary faculty appear to have limited understandings of the nature of librarians' instructional work and expertise. Faculty may therefore often be unaware

---

29. Lars Christiansen, Mindy Stombler, and Lyn Thaxton, "A Report on Librarian-Faculty Relations from a Sociological Perspective," *Journal of Academic Librarianship* 30, no. 2 (March 2004): 117–120, doi:10.1016/j. acalib.2004.01.003.

of the ways that librarians can support students beyond pointing them to specific resources and research tools.

## *Conceptions of Information Literacy and of Librarians' Instructional Roles*

Conceptions of information literacy play a powerful role in how librarians engage in direct instruction and in teaching collaborations. As discussed in Chapter 1, the term "information literacy" has often been understood to describe the mere mechanics of finding information, a view reflected in the perception of information literacy as an "add-on." (Several interviewees whose work was described in Chapter 4 noted the common perception of information literacy as something extra that is tacked onto a course.) Such conceptions of information literacy have been shaped in part by library instruction over the past century, though many librarians have resisted such views of information literacy and of library instruction.

Conveying the relevance of information literacy to course instructors remains a significant challenge for librarians, even when course instructors believe that information literacy is an important part of college education. This is reflected in a number of studies on teaching faculty's approaches to information literacy instruction and their perspectives on the topic. Claire McGuiness interviewed sociology and civil engineering faculty in Ireland and found that most believed that information literacy was important, but expected that students would "pick up" these abilities naturally as long as they were motivated in their academic work. As McGuiness explains, "[t]here was a tacit assumption among faculty that students would somehow absorb and develop the requisite knowledge and skills through the very process of preparing a piece of written coursework, and by applying advice meted out by their supervisors." There was a common view that students' development of information literacy "depends almost entirely on personal interest, individual motivation and innate ability, rather than on the quality and format of the available instruction opportunities."[30] Empirical studies, like those discussed in Chapter 2, illustrate that the view that information literacy development is something that will occur "naturally" does not take into account the complexity of information seeking and use.[31] Literature from composition and rhetoric, in particular that on Writing Across the Curriculum initiatives, often suggests that many faculty hold similar views of writing.

The context-dependent nature of information and writing practices provoke questions about whose responsibility it is to teach information literacy and at what points in college curricula such instruction should occur; this is an issue that will be familiar to writing instructors as well.[32] Both Shelley Gullikson and Laura Saunders found through interviews with teaching faculty that while there is general agreement among teaching faculty that information literacy is important, beliefs about who should teach it often differ.[33] Saunders also found that teaching faculty often place a higher priority on covering content over teaching skills and processes, a reality that also suggests challenges for WAC advocates.[34]

---

30. Claire McGuinness, "What Faculty Think—Exploring the Barriers to Information Literacy Development in Undergraduate Education," *Journal of Academic Librarianship* 32, no. 6 (2006): 577.

31. Andrew Asher, Lynda Duke, and David Green, "The ERIAL Project: Ethnographic Research in Illinois Academic Libraries," *The Academic Commons*, May 17, 2010, http://www.academiccommons.org/2014/09/09/the-erial-project-ethnographic-research-in-illinois-academic-libraries/.; Alison J. Head and Michael B. Eisenberg, *Finding Context: What Today's College Students Say about Conducting Research in the Digital Age* (Project Information Literacy Progress Report, University of Washington's Information School, February 4, 2009), http://projectinfolit.org/images/pdfs/pil_progressreport_2_2009.pdf.; Alison J. Head and Michael B. Eisenberg, *Truth Be Told: How College Students Evaluate and Use Information in the Digital Age*. Project Information Literacy Progress Report (Project Information Literacy, November 1, 2010).

32. Elmborg, "Information Literacy and Writing Across the Curriculum," 68.

33. Shelley Gullikson, "Faculty Perceptions of ACRL's Information Literacy Competency Standards for Higher Education," *Journal of Academic Librarianship* 32, no. 6 (2006): 583–92; Laura Saunders, "Faculty Perspectives on Information Literacy as a Student Learning Outcome," *Journal of Academic Librarianship* 38, no. 4 (July 2012): 226–36, doi:10.1016/j.acalib.2012.06.001.

34. Saunders, "Faculty Perspectives on Information Literacy as a Student Learning Outcome," 227.

While conceptions of information literacy as procedural appear fairly common among teaching faculty, some librarians may share similar perspectives. As noted earlier, since rhetorical and theoretically-informed approaches to library instruction have only recently become more common in librarianship, and although library instruction in the past decade has become significantly more focused on information literacy as a situated practice, most librarians still enter the field with limited instructional training. A significant number of librarians do come to the profession with teaching backgrounds, but a much greater number acquire deeper knowledge of pedagogy through other means such as conferences, workshops, work with colleagues, and on-the-job teaching experience (as do many disciplinary faculty). Thus, the range of librarians' experiences and comfort levels with teaching outside of library tool demonstrations vary widely. This can also contribute to uncertainty about how writing and information literacy instruction might be approached in integrative and complementary ways. Scott Walter's study of librarians' identities as teachers is a good starting point for further reading on this topic.[35]

## Old Ghosts of the Library-Writing Classroom

As I have been arguing, mechanical conceptions of information literacy are likely to limit the potential for librarians and compositionists to work together more fully. Although most instruction librarians would challenge definitions of information literacy that reduce it to mechanics, implementing such an approach is quite challenging in "one-shot" library sessions in which librarians are asked to introduce students to essential library resources in a way that often seems disconnected from the larger course.

In his 2004 article "Writing Information Literacy," Rolf Norgaard also considers common disconnects between the instructional work

---

35. Scott Walter, "Librarians as Teachers: A Qualitative Inquiry into Professional Identity," *College & Research Libraries* 69, no. 1 (January 2008): 51–71.

of librarians and writing instructors. Many of the barriers to dialogue and collaboration that he describes suggest that compositionists' and librarians' past relationships may limit the possibilities we see for our current and future interactions. He describes barriers to partnerships as "old ghosts and new specters" and asserts that, in order for the two professions to work in more collaborative ways, librarians and writing instructors must confront these phantoms:

> If libraries continue to evoke, for writing teachers and their students, images of the quick field trip, the scavenger hunt, the generic, stand-alone tutorial, or the dreary research paper, the fault remains, in large part, rhetoric and composition's failure to adequately theorize the role of libraries and information literacy in its own rhetorical self-understanding and pedagogical practice.[36]

As a rhetorician, Norgaard calls for his profession to engage more actively in reenvisioning its connection to libraries and librarians. As a librarian, I will add that librarians can also become more aware of compositionists' varying perspectives, including their differing understandings of the library and of librarians' relationships to writing instruction. When individuals from both professions develop this fuller awareness, we are better able to address misconceptions about information literacy and writing instruction and to engage in fuller conversations.

The two most notable ghosts that Norgaard mentions are the research paper and fears of plagiarism.[37] This first concern, the traditional research paper, has long been discussed and frequently dreaded by writing instructors, many of whom have convincingly argued that the artificiality of traditional research papers leads to empty and formulaic writing.

---

36. Rolf Norgaard, "Writing Information Literacy: Contributions to a Concept," *Reference & User Services Quarterly* 43, no. 2 (Winter 2003): 124.

37. Rolf Norgaard, "Writing Information Literacy in the Classroom: Pedagogical Enactments and Implications," *Reference User Services Quarterly* 43, no. 3 (2004): 221.

## The Infamous Research Paper

In the field of composition and rhetoric, reservations about research papers became most explicitly recognized around 1982 when Richard Larson published "The 'Research Paper' in the Writing Course: A Non-Form of Writing." This essay helped to spur the debate in writing and rhetoric about the role of such assignments in writing courses. Larson argued that the research paper is an artificial genre that has "no conceptual or procedural identity" and "no distinctly identifiable kind of writing."[38] In claiming to teach the "research paper," Larson argued, "we mislead students about the activities of both research and writing."[39] Though the traditional research paper continues to be a staple of most introductory college writing courses, some writing instructors assign it begrudgingly, while others do not give research assignments, often because of the inauthentic nature of this genre and the "cut-and-paste" approach that students often apply to it.

Reservations about assigning research writing may contribute to a lack of dialogue between librarians and composition instructors, given that the traditional research paper has created perhaps the strongest link between writing courses and library instruction. When instructors do not assign standard research papers, they may see no reason to work with a librarian. Faculty have expressed this view to me and many of my library colleagues in informal conversations. Similarly, Saunders found in faculty interviews that perceptions of information literacy's importance in an instructor's course usually depended on whether students were assigned a research paper.[40] While the association between libraries and

---

38. Richard L. Larson, "The 'Research Paper' in the Writing Course: A Non-Form of Writing," *College English* 44, no. 8 (1982): 813.

39. Ibid., 812.

40. Laura Saunders, "Faculty Perspectives on Information Literacy as a Student Learning Outcome," *Journal of Academic Librarianship* 38, no. 4 (July 2012): 231, doi:10.1016/j.acalib.2012.06.001.

the research paper is logical, the perception that librarians have little to contribute to teaching anything other than the traditional research paper is founded more on the ghosts that Norgaard identifies than on the actual possibilities for collaborative teaching. As reflected in recent discussions of alternative research assignments (which can be found in the professional literature of both composition and information literacy), inquiry- and research-based assignments can take a wide range of forms and can address real audiences and questions.[41]

The "ghosts" and "specters" that often hover over interactions between librarians and writing instructors are not limited to the research paper and plagiarism. Those two issues point to larger concerns about how research and writing are taught. As explored in the previous chapters, formulaic approaches to source-based research are likely to reinforce preconceptions about what information literacy instruction can look like.

Mechanical approaches to teaching about library research are not uncommon, as librarians Melissa Bowles-Terry, Erin Davis, and Wendy Holliday found at their institution through examinations of writing course assignments and curricula, interviews with writing instructors, and analysis of writing and library instruction materials used more broadly by writing instructors and librarians. The instructional practices they observed, which often belied the recursive and complex nature of research and source use, include "the one-shot [library] instructional session, tool-based library demonstration, the Web evaluation checklist, and writing textbooks that provide linear, step-by-step procedures for proper information retrieval."[42] These kinds of teaching practices, Bowles-Terry and her colleagues write, "reinforce the idea that research is about finding the correct amount of the right kind of facts and

---

41. Douglass Brent, "The Research Paper and Why We Should Still Care," *Writing Program Administration* 37, no. 1 (2013): 33–55; Robert Davis and Mark Shadle, "'Building a Mystery': Alternative Research Writing and the Academic Act of Seeking," *College Composition and Communication* 51, no. 3 (2000): 417–66, doi:10.2307/358743; Barbara Fister, "Decode Academy" (keynote presentation, LOEX, Nashville, TN, May 3, 2013), http://homepages.gac.edu/~fister/loex13.pdf.

42. Melissa Bowles-Terry, Erin Davis, and Wendy Holliday, "'Writing Information Literacy' Revisited: Application of Theory to Practice in the Classroom," *Reference & User Services Quarterly* 49, no. 3 (2010), 228.

reporting these facts back to the teacher," rather than about asking and exploring meaningful questions.[43] Their findings are further supported by compositionists Purdy and Walker's examination of instructional materials used in composition classrooms, as was discussed in Chapter 2.[44] Other investigations into research instruction practices further indicate both high school and college educators tend to place little emphasis on research's larger rhetorical purposes.[45]

Such teaching runs counter to the to approach research and writing that most writing instructors and librarians want their students to take, yet these pedagogical strategies are frequently used in both fields. Exploring best practices for teaching about information seeking and use goes hand in hand with the discussion of differing conceptions of information literacy and of librarians' instructional work.

## *"At-Your-Service" Librarianship*

Many librarians strive to address the limited conceptions of information literacy that lie behind mechanical approaches to teaching source-based research, but they must often do so while negotiating ambiguous instructional roles. Differing perspectives among academic librarians of what it means to teach or to identify as an educator are sometimes a source of tension within the profession. On one hand, academic library culture in many respects encourages librarians to embrace

---

43. Ibid., 228.

44. James P. Purdy and Joyce R. Walker, "Liminal Spaces and Research Identity: The Construction of Introductory Composition Students as Researchers," *Pedagogy: Critical Approaches to Teaching Literature, Language, Composition, and Culture* 13, no. 1 (Winter 2013): 9–41.

45. Wendy Holliday and Jim Rogers, "Talking About Information Literacy: The Mediating Role of Discourse in a College Writing Classroom," *portal: Libraries and the Academy* 13, no. 3 (2013): 257–71; Louise Limberg and Olaf Sundin, "Teaching Information Seeking: Relating Information Literacy Education to Theories of Information Behaviour," *Information Research* 12, no. 1 (2006); Barbara Valentine, "The Legitimate Effort in Research Papers: Student Commitment versus Faculty Expectations," *Journal of Academic Librarianship* 27, no. 2 (March 2001): 107–15; Robert A. Schwegler and Linda K. Shamoon, "The Aims and Process of the Research Paper," *College English* 44, no. 8 (1982): 817–24.

their roles as teaching partners with disciplinary faculty. On the other hand, librarianship is often driven by a customer-oriented business model that can reinforce the asymmetrical relationship commonly found between librarians and disciplinary faculty. Though the idea of university education as a business is hardly limited to academic libraries, librarianship's beginnings as a service-oriented profession–in addition to budget cuts that often affect libraries disproportionately–appear to have made academic libraries particularly prone to focusing on customer satisfaction, "added value," and "return on investment" analyses. Such approaches have been described in recent years in terms of the "neoliberal library," whose value is understood more in terms of a capitalist market than in connection to lifelong learning. While it is not within the scope of this chapter to explore in detail the concept of the neoliberal academic library, I will look more closely at one aspect of this broader topic: the influence of an "at-your-service" approach to librarianship that may prevent deeper dialogue and collaboration.[46]

I find it useful here to distinguish between librarianship in the service of teaching and learning and what I am calling an "at-your-service" approach, in which librarians appear subservient to other instructors and limited in their freedom to express and to make use of their own pedagogical perspectives and expertise. I am not suggesting that librarians should not provide service or should not view what libraries offer as services. To the contrary, I believe that service in support of shared goals (like teaching and learning) is key to what librarians do. However, the form that library services (and library instructional services in particular) often take is one of approaching faculty as customers rather than as colleagues. As Yvonne Nalani Meulemans and Allison Carr assert:

---

46. For more discussion on the neoliberal academic library see: Maura Seale, "The Neoliberal Library," in *Information Literacy and Social Justice: Radical Professional Praxis*, ed. Lua Gregory and Shana Higgins (Sacramento, CA: Library Juice Press, 2013), 39–61; Ian Beilin, "Student Success and the Neoliberal Academic Library," *Canadian Journal of Academic Librarianship* 1, no. 1 (2016), http://www.cjal.ca/index.php/capal/article/download/24303.; Chris Bourg, "The Neoliberal Library: Resistance Is Not Futile," *Feral Librarian*, January 16, 2014, https://chrisbourg.wordpress.com/2014/01/16/the-neoliberal-library-resistance-is-not-futile/.ed.

The "customer is always right" attitude is not an effective teaching or collaborative philosophy. This attitude will perpetuate an uneven relationship and not adhere the most important point in Ivey's (2003) behaviors for successful collaboration: mutual respect, tolerance and trust. Also, if instruction librarians fail to engage faculty in a collaborative manner, no amount of marketing or superficial outreach will help to create the partnerships we so desire. When a problematic request is fulfilled, it only ensures that librarians will receive more requests like it.[47]

As Meulemans and Carr contend, the traditional service model of librarianship often works to affirm an understanding of librarians as subservient. This dynamic does not encourage open dialogue or creative planning, and it frequently perpetuates conceptions of information literacy as decontextualized and merely mechanical.

A significant amount of library literature on librarian-faculty relations illustrates that, at least from the perspective of librarians, conditions found to be essential to successful librarian-faculty collaboration (which, as Ivey found, include a shared goal; mutual respect, tolerance, and trust; and ongoing communication) are often not in place.[48] Librarians have repeatedly expressed in surveys and interviews the difficulties of building partnerships, which are tied largely to many faculty's limited views of librarians' work and of what librarians can bring to teaching and learning.[49] However, it is also important to note that many instruction librarians have very positive experiences with collaboration, as is evident in the work of the librarians I interviewed for Chapter 4. Such examples can serve as counter-narratives that challenge the idea that librarians should or must work only in the service of others (rather than collaboratively determining shared goals). Resisting academic and library cultures that have contributed to an unequal librarian-faculty dynamic

---

47. Yvonne Nalani Meulemans and Allison Carr, "Not at Your Service: Building Genuine Faculty-Librarian Partnerships," Reference Services Review 41, no. 1 (2013): 83, doi:10.1108/00907321311300893.

48. Ivey, "Information Literacy."

49. Hardesty, "Faculty Culture and Bibliographic Instruction"; McGuinness, "What Faculty Think–Exploring the Barriers to Information Literacy Development in Undergraduate Education"; Christiansen, Stombler, and Thaxton, "A Report on Librarian-Faculty Relations from a Sociological Perspective."

is a long-term and complex task, but this dynamic does appear to be changing, however gradually.

## Reframing Librarianship in the Service of Teaching and Learning, Reframing Agency

Because the asymmetrical relationship between librarians and disciplinary faculty reflects complex structural and cultural contexts that contribute to circumstances that are beyond any single individual's control, it may be easy to feel powerless in shifting these conditions. But librarians may have more agency to address this imbalance than is sometimes acknowledged in the profession. Heidi Julien and Jen Pecoskie suggest ways that librarians might reconceive their teaching roles and relationships with disciplinary faculty and thus exercise greater agency in those interactions. Reporting on their interviews with instruction librarians, Julien and Pecoskie draw on the concept of "symbolic interactionism" to consider interviewees' experiences with campus hierarchies. Symbolic interactionism, based on the work of sociologist George Herbert Mead, works from the view that "roles and identities are constructed and evolve through social interaction."[50] As Julien and Pecoskie explain, "[i]ndividual conduct is associated with a specific position or set of circumstances, which provide behavioral guidelines, prescriptions, and boundaries" that individuals interpret and which then inform how they behave.[51] Thus, how one interacts in a given environment can be understood in relation to a complex range of social and cultural factors, including how one understands her/his position within that setting.

Among Julien and Pecoskie's key interview findings is that librarians used "deference" discourse (a concept articulated by sociologist

50. Heidi Julien and Jen (J. L.) Pecoskie, "Librarians' Experiences of the Teaching Role: Grounded in Campus Relationships," *Library & Information Science Research* 31, no. 3 (September 2009): 150, doi:10.1016/j.lisr.2009.03.005.; George H. Mead, "A Behavioristic Account of the Significant Symbol," *Journal of Philosophy* 19 (1922): 157–63.

51. Julien and Pecoskie, "Librarians' Experiences of the Teaching Role," 150.

Erving Goffman) in their conversations with faculty.[52] Such language was reflected in librarians' perceptions of faculty's superior status and in librarians' devaluing of their own time and expertise. For example, librarians often described class time given to information literacy instruction as a "gift" from faculty members (though librarians were actually offering a service to those faculty). I have similarly heard many librarians state that they wish an instructor would grant them more time with a class. This wish is understandable, but the focus on how a faculty member has the right to give or withhold often draws attention away from the idea that a librarians' time and energy are just as valuable as those of other educators. Such deferent language suggests that many librarians experience a lower social standing within their campus structures. As Priscilla S. Rogers and Song Mei Lee-Wong note, "[d]eferent communications show an awareness that organizational relationships are asymmetrical in one way or another, if not by an imposed pecking order, then by expertise and experience."[53]

At the same time that campus hierarchies are often perceptible and real, deferent language and an unquestioning acceptance of one's lower social rank may help to uphold that structure. Julien and Pecoskie observed in their librarian interviews that the lack of respect from teaching faculty that some study participants experienced "was also supported by librarians' self-positioning as defeated, passive, dependent, and subordinate to teaching faculty."[54] Though the ways in which librarians and faculty interact are contextual and vary considerably, Julien and Pecoskie's findings suggest that there is a general tendency in librarianship to speak and to behave in ways that devalue one's own

---

52. The concepts of deference discourse and deference behavior were first articulated by Erving Goffman, as Julien and Pecoskie note. See: Ibid., 151; Erving Goffman, *Interaction Ritual: Essays on Face-to-Face Interaction* (New Brunswick, NJ: Transaction Publishers, 1967).

53. Priscilla S. Rogers and Song Me9 Lee-Wong, "Reconceptualizing Politeness to Accommodate Dynamic Tensions in Subordinate-to-Superior Reporting," *Journal of Business and Technical Communication* 17, no. 4 (October 2003): 397.

54. Julien and Pecoskie, "Librarians' Experiences of the Teaching Role," 152..

contributions, perspectives, or priorities in favor of those of disciplinary faculty. While the desire to help others is among the important values and strengths of librarians, the instructional services that librarians offer to teaching faculty often require a balancing and negotiating of instructional goals and approaches. In many cases librarians, in wanting to provide valued services that do not disturb a faculty member's own approaches and perceived preferences, may sometimes hold back from offering pedagogical perspectives and approaches that would be beneficial to students. As Julien and Pecoskie imply, and as Meulemans and Carr argue, hierarchical relationships between disciplinary faculty and librarians frequently present challenges to approaching information literacy instruction in more nuanced ways. When such a dynamic is in place, it is often the instructor who defines what librarian-led instruction looks like. This contrasts with course-integrated instruction that is a collaborative effort to which the librarian brings specialized knowledge, skills, and pedagogical approaches.

Julien and Pecoskie's research suggests that librarians, along with other educators, can benefit from critically examining the unwritten and often invisible guidelines and prescriptions under which we operate. For example, the tendency to devalue librarians' expertise and time in relation to that of teaching faculty may support a hierarchical structure and limit the possibilities for developing integrative approaches to information literacy instruction. Librarians, by strengthening awareness of how the institutional structures in which they work influence their behaviors and actions, can better position themselves to challenge conditions in libraries and in higher education that limit the potential for fostering student learning. Though I have focused here on the library profession because of the particular position librarians experience in relation to disciplinary faculty, this might also be said for compositionists and other educators. I will return to the relevance of critical practice to writing instruction in the subsequent section.

Efforts to increase awareness of the role of institutional structures, along with other factors like professional roles and interpersonal dynamics, may call to mind the concept of "reflective practice" which has been explored by educators such as Stephen Brookfield and Donald Schön.[55] For Brookfield, reflective practice begins with recognizing and examining assumptions while remaining cognizant of "[t]he cultural, psychological and political complexities of learning, and the ways in which power complicates all human relationships."[56] Particularly important to him is identifying and reflecting on "paradigmatic assumptions" that usually operate outside the awareness of an individual or a group. These paradigmatic assumptions, Brookfield writes, are "the hardest of all assumptions to uncover," for

> [t]hey are the structuring assumptions we use to order the world into fundamental categories. Usually we don't even recognize them as assumptions, even after they've been pointed out to us. Instead we insist that they're objectively valid renderings of reality, the facts as we know them to be true. [57]

Julien and Pecoskie's interviews suggest that, for librarians, these assumptions may sometimes include believing a course instructor's time to be more valuable than one's own time, without considering that librarians offer the gifts of their own time, energy, and expertise. Such beliefs can become so ingrained in how an individual or a service profession generally thinks that it operates outside of one's awareness. And it can play a powerful role in how individuals and groups interact, as well as in the cultures and norms that develop within and across groups. As Pecoskie and Julien's work suggest, this has important implications for teaching partnerships in which librarians are involved.

Librarian Anne-Marie Deitering made a similar point in a LOEX keynote presentation that explored the value of reflective practice for instruction librarians. Along with her colleague Kate Gronemeyer,

---

55. Stephen Brookfield, *Becoming a Critically Reflective Teacher*, 1st ed, The Jossey-Bass Higher and Adult Education Series (San Francisco: Jossey-Bass, 1995); Donald A. Schön, *Educating the Reflective Practitioner* (San Francisco: Jossey-Bass, 1987).

56. Brookfield, *Becoming a Critically Reflective Teacher*, 1.

57. Ibid., 2.

Deitering conducted interviews with instruction librarians about their individual teaching practices (which centered mainly on one-shot teaching). Interviewees often interpreted difficulties in collaborating with other teachers as indications that they, as librarians, had done something wrong. These librarians appeared to take full responsibility for an instruction session being less than successful, while overlooking or minimizing other contextual factors that were beyond their control. Deitering identified this tendency as reflective of the kinds of assumptions that Brookfield encourages educators to question. These include assumptions like "a good librarian will fix any problem related to her students' learning in the moment." Such a narrative, according to Deitering,

> lets me focus all of my work to fix the problem on me and my own teaching, on developing a big enough bag of tricks to respond to any situation. And I don't deal with the underlying issues with the course instructor—about the power relationships between us or about the things they are doing that sabotage their students' learning.[58]

In reality, Deitering asserts,

> there is a lot of basic stuff out of our [librarians'] control. (true for all teachers, but especially for librarians). Taken together with [the theme of] power [that surfaced in these interviews] ... we couldn't help coming away with the idea that despite this, we instruction librarians [] take an awful lot of responsibility on ourselves.[59]

Deitering went on to describe how many interviewees interpreted things they perceived to have gone wrong in their teaching, in particular events that were out of their control (and in some cases in the control of the respective course instructor), as examples of their own failure. This

---

58. Anne-Marie Deitering, "Reflections on Reflection. Or, How I Learned to Stop Worrying and Embrace the Meta" (keynote presentation at LOEX, Denver, Colorado, May 1, 2015), http://info-fetishist.org/2015/05/01/loex2015/.

59. Ibid.

suggests a tendency to overlook external conditions that have a profound impact on any teaching context and to be overly critical of one's own teaching. This is not to say that all librarians have this inclination, or that teachers from other fields do not. But the fact that it was a common theme in Deitering and Gronemeyer's interviews suggests that there is likely a tendency among librarians toward such a mindset. And yet, the unique conditions of teaching stand-alone library sessions are reason enough to appreciate the constraints it presents to any instructor.

The tendency to minimize the role of external conditions in a library session likely contributes to the feeling of disempowerment many librarians experience in relation to their teaching and their institutional position. When larger structural and material conditions that affect library instruction receive limited attention, many librarians may focus more heavily on what they could have done differently. Deitering asks librarians to consider instead the broader circumstances that affect their teaching as they engage in a reflective practice of looking both inward and outward. Drawing on Brookfield's work, Deitering invites librarians "to identify and question the assumptions that lie under the surface of our practice," particularly "hegemonic assumptions" that might "seem fine, but can cause us to be complicit in our own oppression."[60] ("Oppression" seems to me a strong word to use here, but I agree with Deitering's overall sentiment.) This is not to say that librarians cannot strengthen their teaching and their potential for building teaching partnerships by critiquing their own instruction. It is to say that reflective and open critique of any pedagogical practice must look at the broader contexts and circumstances that influence teaching and learning. One important piece of that context is institutional structures and their potential influences on teaching and learning within and outside of the classroom.

The tendency of many librarians to find fault with their own teaching is further evident in Hardesty's earlier analysis of the literature on librarian-faculty relations. He observed that most library literature on

---

60. Ibid.; Brookfield, *Becoming a Critically Reflective Teacher.*

faculty resistance to collaboration implies (or asserts) that the main solution is for librarians to take more initiative to involve faculty.[61] Though Hardesty's article was written in 1995, this theme remains apparent in much of the library literature today on building relationships with faculty. Far less attention is given to the larger causes and structural issues behind this dynamic or to possibilities for challenging what Brookfield might call "hegemonic assumptions" (for example, that the burden and responsibility is and must be entirely on librarians to make collaboration happen, or that if librarians are not successful in these efforts they have done something incorrectly). Nonetheless, works like those of Deitering and Gronemeyer and Meulemans and Carr indicate that another perspective is receiving more attention and helping to shift conversations about librarians' instructional roles in productive ways. Many writing instructors have engaged in similar conversations about their professional roles. As I consider shortly, such conversations often suggest the value of examining paradigmatic assumptions such as those that Brookfield describes.

## Reexamining Institutional Positions, Reexamining the Language of Writing and Information Literacy

In many respects, compositionists and librarians may relate to one another's experiences of existing on the periphery of higher education. Academic rank can vary considerably among both writing instructors and librarians; many, though not all, compositionists have contingent and often part-time positions, and while most librarian positions are full-time, librarians' academic ranks vary considerably from institution to institution.[62] At the same time, the general differences between

---

61. Hardesty, "Faculty Culture and Bibliographic Instruction," 361.

62. Some library positions are classified as faculty rank, while others are described as academic professional or as staff positions. Although faculty status is sometimes considered a means of placing librarians on a more equal footing with disciplinary faculty, the library literature suggests that faculty status does not remove the perception of librarians as being something other than peers. Debates about the legitimacy and effects of faculty status

each professions' everyday work and positions may help to explain the disconnect that often occurs between them. While most compositionists' teaching aligns more closely with the work of other teaching faculty, librarians' job responsibilities and work structures tend to be distinct from that of most teaching faculty.

While the ways that librarians and compositionists are affected by hierarchical structures are largely distinct, some of the sources of these circumstances are similar. Perhaps the most apparent of these circumstances is the common misunderstandings that writing and information literacy are simple skills. A key to challenging related misconceptions about the work of compositionists and instruction librarians is examining the language used to describe writing and information literacy. Rose makes this argument in relation to English composition programs in his essay "The Language of Exclusion." After drawing connections between the generally low status of writing instructors and misconceptions of writing development and practice as simple skills, he contends that the first step that compositionists can take to redress the misunderstandings about writing instruction "is to consider the language institutions use when they discuss writing."[63] Rose continues, "We can begin by affirming a rich model of written language development and production."[64] This model can be a holistic one that "honor[s] the cognitive and emotional and situational dimensions of language" and which "aid[s] us in

---

on academic librarianship have been extensive, but are not the focus of this chapter. For fuller discussions of the role of librarians as teachers see: Lisa G. O'Connor, "Librarians' Professional Struggles in the Information Age: A Critical Analysis of Information Literacy" (PhD diss., Kent State University, 2006); Susan Ariew, "How We Got Here: A Historical Look at the Academic Teaching Library and the Role of the Teaching Librarian," *Communications in Information Literacy* 8, no. 2 (September 2014): 208–24.2006. For more detailed examinations of librarians faculty status see: Danielle Bodrero Hoggan, "Faculty Status for Librarians in Higher Education," *portal: Libraries and the Academy* 3, no. 3 (2003): 431–45, and Janet Swan Hill, "Wearing Our Own Clothes: Librarians as Faculty," *Journal of Academic Librarianship* 20, no. 2 (1994): 71–76.

63. Rose, "The Language of Exclusion," 342.

64. Ibid., 357.

understanding what we can observe as well as what we can only infer."[65] Such a view of literacy development challenges the notion that writing and information literacy are rote skills to be learned prior to more "rigorous" study.

One can see in Rose's description of writing development as cognitive, emotional, and situational, strong parallels with the language of the WPA *Framework* and the ACRL *Framework*, documents that illustrate the interconnections between what compositionists and librarians seek to foster. Just as these frameworks are intended to communicate the contextual and rhetorical nature of writing and information practices in ways that may positively influence discussions about and approaches to writing and information literacy instruction, Rose asks his colleagues to help shift understandings of writing instruction through dialogue with others: "When discussions and debates reveal a more reductive model of language, we must call time out and reestablish the terms of the argument."[66] For Rose, this is essential to addressing misconceptions about writing development and writing pedagogies, and ultimately to repositioning compositionists' roles within their institutions. This argument can be extended to librarians.

Efforts to realize such change can begin with our own reflective practices. As Rose asserts, writing instructors can "rigorously examine our own teaching and see what model of language lies beneath it."[67] For Rose, this means asking questions such as:

> What linguistic assumptions are cued when we face freshman writers? Are they compatible with the assumptions that are cued when we think about our own writing or the writing of those we read for pleasure? Do we too operate with the bifurcated mind that for too long characterized the teaching of "remedial" students and that is still reflected in the language of our institutions?[68]

---

65. Ibid., 353.

66. Ibid., 357.

67. Ibid.

68. Ibid.

Similar questions about information literacy are relevant to both compositionists and librarians. What assumptions do we make about students as researchers, or about their conceptions or approaches to seeking and using information? What do research assignments and related instruction imply about the purposes of seeking and using sources? Are there disconnects between how we represent information seeking and use and how we hope for students to engage in these activities, or between the information practices we ask students to engage with and those that we find meaningful in our personal and professional lives? Do our instructional approaches suggest that information seeking and use are more matters of procedure than rhetorically and socially situated activities? These questions illustrate that compositionists and librarians can look both outward and inward when considering how writing and information literacy can be approached in integrative ways and how we can support such work in our own roles. They are also the type of questions one might ask when examining the sorts of paradigmatic assumptions that Brookfield describes, "structuring assumptions we use to order the world into fundamental categories," but which may not always serve us well.[69]

As compositionists and librarians consider our teaching practices along with the educational systems in which we work, librarian Heidi L.M. Jacobs' description of "reflective pedagogical praxis" may be particularly useful. Jacobs' work appears to be influenced by the concept of "critical practice" described by those like Brookfield, though she does not make explicit reference to this body of literature. Writing to a librarian audience, Jacobs suggests that in examining teaching practices and educational systems relationally, librarians might also "ask new questions of [librarianship] and foster creative, reflective and critical habits of mind regarding pedagogical praxis."[70] She states, "If we are going to address the issues of librarians' roles within educational endeavors

---

69. Ibid., 2.

70. Heidi L. M. Jacobs, "Information Literacy and Reflective Pedagogical Praxis," *Journal of Academic Librarianship* 34, no. 3 (May 2008): 256, doi:10.1016/j.acalib.2008.03.009.

systemically, we, as a discipline, need to foster reflective, critical habits of mind regarding pedagogical praxis within ourselves, our libraries, and our campuses."[71]

Fittingly, Jacobs' interest in applying a "reflective pedagogical praxis" to librarianship is informed by work in composition and rhetoric and by her own closely related work in literacy studies. In describing "reflective pedagogical praxis," Jacobs draws on the writing of literacy studies scholars Stenberg and Lee, who liken the act of reading a text to examining one's teaching practice:

> ...[C]ritically reading our teaching in the same careful way we've learned to engage scholarly and literary texts in English studies is crucial. That is, if pedagogy is at once a means and object of inquiry, we need to develop ways of studying our teaching, of reading our pedagogical interactions and our pedagogical development (exploration, critique, revision) as texts.[72]

Given the centrality of inquiry to both information literacy and writing, this conception of teaching will likely resonate with many in both professions. Though Jacobs focuses on the implications of this statement for librarians, she also considers the relevance of Stenberg and Lee's ideas to librarian-faculty dialogue. Here Jacobs quotes Rolf Norgaard, who encouraged reflective dialogue between librarians and compositionists: "[w]e would do well to listen attentively to each other's voices... We need each other more than both of us may think."[73]

This book explores how compositionists' and librarians' can better understand how our work intersects and how it can function in more complementary ways. While we may be able to do our basic jobs without one another, the ideas, research, and collaborative projects explored throughout this book illustrate how our work is deepened—and perhaps also made more enjoyable—by fuller conversations and partnerships. In

---

71. Ibid.

72. Shari Stenberg and Amy Lee, "Developing Pedagogies: Learning the Teaching of English," *College English* 64, no. 3 (2002): 328.

73. Jacobs, "Information Literacy and Reflective Pedagogical Praxis," 261.

the next and final chapter I consider how these themes and topics might help to strengthen and further the connections between our professions.

# Chapter 6

## LOOKING BACK, LOOKING FORWARD

Many compositionists and librarians are familiar with the possibilities and challenges of building campus teaching partnerships. The similarities between their professional histories and institutional positions suggest reason for joining efforts, at the same time that they may help us to recognize disconnects that often exist between our professions and sometimes our approaches to teaching. This book is based on the premise that compositionists and librarians are better positioned to collaborate on individual, programmatic, and institutional levels when we are aware of and can talk together about our teaching practices and experiences, our institutional positions, the histories and structures that have shaped our work, and the implications that these experiences and circumstances have for partnership.

While there are clearly challenges to growing the connections between our fields, the potential rewards are much greater. I have sought to explore intersections between our work from various angles in each of the preceding chapters. These connections are evident from educational research on writing and information literacy development (Chapter 2), professional documents like the WPA and ACRL frameworks (Chapter 3), compositionist-librarian collaborations (Chapter 4), and similar professional histories and experiences with our instructional and institutional roles (Chapter 5). I have also argued that the concept of reflective practice offers a powerful lens through which to explore the realities and possibilities for our work as individual teachers and as a larger community of educators.

Despite these powerful links between compositionists' and librarians' pedagogical work, the tendency in academia for people to feel overcommitted, time-deficient, and pressured to produce scholarship with relative speed is enough to make dialogue and collaboration difficult. Limited knowledge of one another's professions, and pedagogical experiences and perspectives present additional barriers to library-writing program collaborations. Fortunately, those barriers seem to become more penetrable as conversations among compositionists and librarians expand and as more individuals from both fields recognize the commonalities between our work. These conversations are helping us recognize and address the obstacles that still stand in the way of meaningful collaboration.

The topics explored throughout this book present opportunities for exploring the connections between our work and how we might continue to build mutually supportive relationships. Dialogue is crucial to that larger goal. More specifically, we need more conversations about:

- our common ground, particularly in relation to our instructional goals, teaching experiences, and pedagogical approaches (documents like the ACRL and WPA frameworks have been powerful means of opening such thought)
- where/how our teaching goals and ways of working with students diverge, and how our unique knowledge and experiences can function complementarily
- how we support students in exploring questions and using sources (both in general ways and through specific pedagogies, programs, and services)
- challenges we see students face with inquiry-based processes (including when completing research assignments), and how we do or might respond to those difficulties
- our unique areas of expertise and institutional positioning and how these can work in complementary ways
- how our teaching roles and our institutional positions affect the possibilities and the limitations of supporting students in

developing as writers, researchers, and engaged and informed world citizens

Along with such conversations we can also consider characteristics that foster meaningful partnerships, which as Ruth Ivey's and my interviews indicate, include:

- a shared and understood goal
- mutual respect, tolerance, and trust
- competence for the task at hand
- engagement in ongoing dialogue[1]

In bringing to our conversations a conscious intention to cultivate these qualities in our relationships, we are better able to listen and to explore the possibilities that collaboration, in its many potential forms, might enable.

Experiences from the Writing Across the Curriculum movement–through which many compositionists have worked with educators across academic disciplines–may be particularly informative to our larger programmatic and curricular efforts. Lessons from WAC programs include:

- the importance of non-hierarchical environments that foster open dialogue, while discouraging top-down approaches (through which uniform approaches are often mandated and may communicate the wrong message about intentions to support teaching and learning)
- sensitivity and responsiveness to the local environments and conditions, which become particularly important when extending a collaboration beyond the work of just two partners

---

1. Ruth Ivey, "Information Literacy: How Do Librarians and Academics Work in Partnership to Deliver Effective Learning Programs?", *Australian Academic & Research Libraries* 34, no. 2 (June 2003): 102.

- respect and appreciation for the agency and the unique pedagogical perspectives and approaches of each party, alongside an openness to sharing those perspectives and approaches

These approaches are, of course, much easier to list than to enact, but identifying and articulating how we seek to engage in dialogue and collaboration is, I believe, a powerful starting point for that work.

All of these approaches can be fostered through critical reflection on our own teaching from a variety of vantage points. As discussed in Chapter 5, Heidi L.M. Jacobs describes such an approach in terms of "reflective pedagogical praxis," a process of "ask[ing] new questions" and "foster[ing] creative, reflective and critical habits of mind regarding pedagogical praxis" within and beyond our own professions.[2] As literary studies scholars Shari Stenberg and Amy Lee discuss, pedagogy can be approached as "at once a means and object of inquiry" that requires "develop[ing] ways of studying our teaching, of reading our pedagogical interactions and our pedagogical development (exploration, critique, revision) as texts."[3] While such reflective praxis may often begin as a solitary activity, it can also expand to teaching partnerships. Through both individual and collective reflection, compositionists and librarians can explore the ways that, as Rolf Norgaard suggested in 2004 in exploring the pedagogical potentials of "writing information literacy," "we can benefit from each other more than we may imagine."[4]

---

2. Heidi L. M. Jacobs, "Information Literacy and Reflective Pedagogical Praxis," *Journal of Academic Librarianship* 34, no. 3 (May 2008): 256, doi:10.1016/j.acalib.2008.03.009.

3. Shari Stenberg and Amy Lee, "Developing Pedagogies: Learning the Teaching of English," *College English* 64, no. 3 (2002): 328.

4. Rolf Norgaard, "Writing Information Literacy in the Classroom: Pedagogical Enactments and Implications," *Reference User Services Quarterly* 43, no. 3 (2004): 226.

# BIBLIOGRAPHY

Albert, Michelle, and Caroline Sinkinson. "Composing Information Literacy: A Pedagogical Partnership Between Rhet/
Comp and Library Faculty." Savannah, Georgia, September
25, 2015. http://digitalcommons.georgiasouthern.edu/
gaintlit/2015/2015/74/.

————. "Composing Information Literacy through Pedagogical
Partnerships." In *The Future Scholar: Researching & Teaching
the Frameworks for Writing and Information Literacy*, edited by
Randall McClure and James P. Purdy, 111–29. Medford, NJ:
Information Today, 2016.

American Library Association. *Presidential Committee on Information
Literacy: Final Report*, January 10, 1989. http://www.ala.org/
acrl/publications/whitepapers/presidential.

Apple, Michael W. *Official Knowledge: Democratic Education in a Conservative Age*. New York: Routledge, 1993.

Ariew, Susan. "How We Got Here: A Historical Look at the Academic Teaching Library and the Role of the Teaching Librarian." *Communications in Information Literacy* 8, no. 2 (September
2014): 208–24.

Asher, Andrew. "Search Epistemology: Teaching Students about
Information Discovery." In *Not Just Where to Click: Teach-
ing Students How to Think about Information*, edited by Troy
A. Swanson and Heather Jagman, 139–54. Publications in

Librarianship, 68. Chicago: Association of College and Research Libraries, 2015.

Asher, Andrew, Lynda Duke, and David Green. "The ERIAL Project: Ethnographic Research in Illinois Academic Libraries." *The Academic Commons*, May 17, 2010. http://www.academic-commons.org/2014/09/09/the-erial-project-ethnographic-research-in-illinois-academic-libraries/.

Association of College and Research Libraries. *Framework for Information Literacy for Higher Education*. 2015. http://www.ala.org/acrl/standards/ilframework.

Bazerman, Charles, and David R. Russell, eds. *Writing Selves/Writing Societies: Research from Activity Perspectives*. Perspectives on Writing, an Electronic Books Series. Fort Collins, CO: WAC Clearinghouse, 2003.

Bean, John C. *Engaging Ideas: The Professor's Guide to Integrating Writing, Critical Thinking, and Active Learning in the Classroom*. 2nd ed. The Jossey-Bass Higher and Adult Education Series. San Francisco: Jossey-Bass, 2011.

Beilin, Ian. "Student Success and the Neoliberal Academic Library." *Canadian Journal of Academic Librarianship* 1, no. 1 (January 28, 2016). http://www.cjal.ca/index.php/capal/article/view/24303.

Bergmann, Linda S., and Janet Zepernick. "Disciplinarity and Transfer: Students' Perceptions of Learning to Write." *WPA: Writing Program Administration* 31, no. 1–2 (2007): 124–49.

Berlin, James A. *Writing Instruction in Nineteenth-Century American Colleges*. Studies in Writing & Rhetoric. Carbondale: Southern Illinois University Press, 1984.

Block, Haskell M., and Sidney Mattis. "The Research Paper: A Co-Operative Approach." *College English* 13, no. 4 (1952): 212–215.

Bourg, Chris. "The Neoliberal Library: Resistance Is Not Futile." *Feral Librarian*, January 16, 2014. https://chrisbourg.wordpress.com/2014/01/16/the-neoliberal-library-resistance-is-not-futile/.

Bowles-Terry, Melissa, Erin Davis, and Wendy Holliday. "'Writing Information Literacy' Revisited: Application of Theory to Practice in the Classroom." *Reference & User Services Quarterly* 49, no. 3 (2010): 225–30.

Bergmann, Linda S., and Janet Zepernick. "Disciplinarity and Transfer: Students' Perceptions of Learning to Write," *WPA: Writing Program Administration* 31, no. 1–2 (2007): 124-49.

Brent, Douglass. "The Research Paper and Why We Should Still Care." *Writing Program Administration* 33, no. 1 (2013): 33–53.

Brookfield, Stephen. *Becoming a Critically Reflective Teacher.* 1st ed. The Jossey-Bass Higher and Adult Education Series. San Francisco: Jossey-Bass, 1995.

Chiseri-Strater, Elizabeth. *Academic Literacies: The Public and Private Discourse of University Students.* Portsmouth, NH: Boynton/Cook, 1991.

Christiansen, Lars, Mindy Stombler, and Lyn Thaxton. "A Report on Librarian-Faculty Relations from a Sociological Perspective." *The Journal of Academic Librarianship* 30, no. 2 (March 2004): 116–21. doi:10.1016/j.acalib.2004.01.003.

The Coalition on the Academic Workforce. "A Portrait of Part-Time Faculty Members," June 2012. http://www.academicworkforce.org/CAW_portrait_2012.pdf.

Corso, Gail S., Sandra Weiss, and Tiffany McGregor. "Information Literacy: A Story of Collaboration and Cooperation between the Writing Program Coordinator and Colleagues 2003-2010." Presentaton at the National Conference on the Council of Writing Program Administrators, Philadelphia, PA, July 16, 2010.

Costa, Arthur L., and Bena Kallick, eds. *Learning and Leading with Habits of Mind: 16 Essential Characteristics for Success.* Alexandria, VA: Association for Supervision and Curriculum Development, 2008.

Council of Writing Program Administrators. "WPA Outcomes Statement for First-Year Composition (3.0)," July 17, 2014. http://wpacouncil.org/positions/outcomes.html.

Council of Writing Program Administrators, National Council of Teachers of English, and National Writing Project. *Framework for Success in Postsecondary Writing.* 2011. http://wpacouncil.org/files/framework-for-success-postsecondary-writing.pdf.

Davis, Robert, and Mark Shadle. "'Building a Mystery': Alternative Research Writing and the Academic Act of Seeking." *College Composition and Communication* 51, no. 3 (2000): 417–466. doi:10.2307/358743.

Deitering, Anne-Marie. "Reflections on Reflection. Or, How I Learned to Stop Worrying and Embrace the Meta." Keynote presentation at LOEX 2015, Denver, CO, May 1, 2015. http://info-fetishist.org/2015/05/01/loex2015/.

Detmering, Robert, and Anna Marie Johnson. "'Research Papers Have Always Seemed Very Daunting': Information Literacy Narratives and the Student Research Experience." *portal: Libraries and the Academy* 12, no. 1 (2012): 5–22.

Dewey, John. *Democracy and Education.* New York: Macmillan, 1916.

Downs, Douglas, and Elizabeth Wardle. "Teaching about Writing, Righting Misconceptions: (Re)envisioning 'First-Year Composition' as 'Introduction to Writing Studies.'" *College Composition and Communication* 58, no. 4 (2007): 552–84.

Elmborg, James. "Critical Information Literacy: Implications for Instructional Practice." *Journal of Academic Librarianship* 32, no. 2 (2006): 192–99.

Elmborg, James K. "Information Literacy and Writing Across the Curriculum: Sharing the Vision." *Reference User Services Quarterly* 31, no. 1 (2003): 68–80.

———. "Locating the Center: Libraries, Writing Centers, and Information Literacy." *The Writing Lab Newsletter* 30, no. 6 (2006): 7–11.

ERIAL Project. "Ethnographic Research in Illinois Academic Libraries: Methodology," 2016. www.erialproject.org/project-details/methodology/.

Fister, Barbara. "Decode Academy." Keynote presentation at LOEX, Nashville, TN, May 3, 2013. http://homepages.gac.edu/~fister/loex13.pdf.

Forte, Andrea. "The New Information Literate: Open Collaboration and Information Production in Schools." *International Journal of Computer-Supported Collaborative Learning* 10, no. 1 (2015): 35–51. doi:10.1007/s11412-015-9210-6.

Galvin, Jeanne. "Information Literacy and Integrative Learning." *College & Undergraduate Libraries* 13, no. 3 (2006): 25-51. doi:10.1300/J106v13n03-03.

Gibson, Craig. "Research Skills Across the Curriculum: Connections with Writing-Across-the-Curriculum." In *Writing-Across-the-Curriculum and the Academic Library: A Guide for Librarians, Instructors, and Writing Program Directors*, edited by Jean Sheridan, 55–69. Westport, CT: Greenwood, 1995.

Goffman, Erving. *Interaction Ritual: Essays on Face-to-Face Interaction.* New Brunswick, NJ: Transaction Publishers, 1967.

Green, Dave. "The ERIAL Project: Findings, Ideas, and Tools to Advance Your Library." Conference Paper Summary. Association of College and Research Libraries, 2013. http://www.ala.org/acrl/sites/ala.org.acrl/files/content/conferences/confsandpreconfs/2013/papers/Green_summary.pdf.

Gross, Melissa, and Don Latham. "Undergraduate Perceptions of Information Literacy: Defining, Attaining, and Self-Assessing Skills." *College & Research Libraries* 70, no. 4 (2009): 336–50.

———. "What's Skill Got to Do with It?: Information Literacy Skills and Self-Views of Ability among First-Year College Students." *Journal of the American Society for Information Science and Technology* 63, no. 3 (2012): 574–83. doi:10.1002/asi.21681.

———. "Experiences with and Perceptions of Information: A Phenomenographic Study of First-Year College Students." *Library Quarterly* 81, no. 2 (2011): 161–86. doi:10.1086/658867.

Gullikson, Shelley. "Faculty Perceptions of ACRL's Information Literacy Competency Standards for Higher Education." *Journal of Academic Librarianship* 32, no. 6 (2006): 583–92.

Hardesty, Larry. "Faculty Culture and Bibliographic Instruction: An Exploratory Analysis." *Library Trends* 44, no. 2 (1995): 339–67.

Harrington, Susanmarie, Dan De Santo, and Charlotte J. Mehrtens. "Getting WILD: Writing and Information Literacy in the Disciplines." Savannah, Georgia, 2015. http://digitalcommons.georgiasouthern.edu/gaintlit/2015/2015/74/.

Hatano, Giyoo, and Kayoko Inagaki. "Two Courses of Expertise." In *Child Development and Education in Japan*, edited by H. W. Stevenson, H. Azuma, and K. Hakuta, 262–72. A Series of Books in Psychology. New York: W. H. Freeman/Times Books/ Henry Holt & Co., 1986.

Head, Alison J., and Michael B. Eisenberg. *Finding Context: What Today's College Students Say about Conducting Research in the Digital Age*. Project Information Literacy Progress Report. University of Washington, Information School, February 4, 2009. http://projectinfolit.org/images/pdfs/pil_progressreport_2_2009.pdf.

Head, Alison J., and Michael B. Eisenberg. *Truth Be Told: How College Students Evaluate and Use Information in the Digital Age.* Project Information Literacy Progress Report. Project Information Literacy, 2010.

Hill, Janet Swan. "Wearing Our Own Clothes: Librarians as Faculty." *The Journal of Academic Librarianship* 20, no. 2 (1994): 71–76.

Hoggan, Danielle Bodrero. "Faculty Status for Librarians in Higher Education." *portal: Libraries and the Academy* 3, no. 3 (2003): 431–45.

Holliday, Wendy, and Jim Rogers. "Talking About Information Literacy: The Mediating Role of Discourse in a College Writing Classroom." *portal: Libraries and the Academy* 13, no. 3 (2013): 257–71.

Hook, Sheril. "Teaching Librarians and Writing Center Professionals in Collaboration: Complementary Practices." In *Centers for Learning: Writing Centers and Libraries in Collaboration,* edited by James K. Elmborg and Sheril Hook. Publications in Librarianship, 58. Chicago: Association of College and Research Libraries, 2005.

Howard, Rebecca Moore. "A Plagiarism Pentimento." *Journal of Teaching Writing* 11, no. 3 (1992): 233-45.

Howard, Rebecca Moore, Tricia Serviss, and Tanya K. Rodrigue. "Writing from Sources, Writing from Sentences." *Writing and Pedagogy* 2, no. 2 (2010): 177–92.

Ivey, Ruth. "Information Literacy: How Do Librarians and Academics Work in Partnership to Deliver Effective Learning Programs?" *Australian Academic & Research Libraries* 34, no. 2 (June 2003): 100-113.

Jacobs, Heidi L. M. "Information Literacy and Reflective Pedagogical Praxis." *Journal of Academic Librarianship* 34, no. 3 (May 2008): 256–62. doi:10.1016/j.acalib.2008.03.009.

Jamieson, Sandra, and Rebecca Moore Howard. "Sentence-Mining: Uncovering the Amount of Reading and Reading Comprehension in College Writers' Researched Writing." In *The New Digital Scholar: Exploring and Enriching the Research and Writing Practices of NextGen Students*, edited by Randall McClure and James P. Purdy, 111–33. ASIS&T Monograph Series. Silver Spring, MD: American Society for Information Science and Technology, 2013.

Jansen, Bernard J., and Amanda Spink. "How are We Searching the World Wide Web? A Comparison of Nine Search Engine Transaction Logs." *Information Processing & Management* 42, no. 1 (2006): 248–63.

Julien, Heidi, and Jen (J. L.) Pecoskie. "Librarians' Experiences of the Teaching Role: Grounded in Campus Relationships." *Library & Information Science Research* 31, no. 3 (September 2009): 149–54. doi:10.1016/j.lisr.2009.03.005.

Knapp, Patricia B. *The Monteith College Library Experiment*. New York: Scarecrow Press, 1966.

Knapper, Arno F. "Good Writing–a Shared Responsibility." *Journal of Business Communication* 15, no. 2 (Winter 1978): 23–27.

Kuglitsch, Rebecca Z. "Teaching for Transfer: Reconciling the Framework with Disciplinary Information Literacy." *portal: Libraries and the Academy* 15, no. 3 (2015): 457–70.

Larson, Richard L. "The 'Research Paper' in the Writing Course: A Non-Form of Writing." *College English* 44, no. 8 (1982): 811–816.

Laurent, Michaël R., and Tim J. Vickers. "Seeking Health Information Online: Does Wikipedia Matter?" *Journal of the American Medical Informatics Association* 16, no. 4 (2009): 471–79.

Lewis, Alison M., ed. *Questioning Library Neutrality: Essays from Progressive Librarian*. Duluth, MN: Library Juice Press, 2008.

Limberg, Louise. "Experiencing Information Seeking and Learning: A Study of the Interaction between Two Phenomena." *Information Research: An International Electronic Journal* 5, no. 1 (1999): 50–67.

Limberg, Louise, and Olaf Sundin. "Teaching Information Seeking: Relating Information Literacy Education to Theories of Information Behaviour." *Information Research* 12, no. 1 (2006). http://www.informationr.net/ir/12-1/paper280.html.

Mackey, Thomas P., and Trudi Jacobson. *Metaliteracy: Reinventing Information Literacy to Empower Learners*. Chicago : ALA Neal-Schuman, American Library Association, 2014.

Margolin, Stephanie, and Wendy Hayden. "Beyond Mechanics: Reframing the Pedagogy and Development of Information Literacy Teaching Tools." *Journal of Academic Librarianship* 41, no. 5 (2015): 602–12. doi:10.1016/j.acalib.2015.07.001.

Mazziotti, Donna, and Teresa Grettano. "'Hanging Together': Collaboration between Information Literacy and Writing Programs Based on the ACRL Standards and the WPA Outcomes." In *ACRL 2011 Conference Papers*, 180–90. Chicago: Association of College and Research Libraries, 2011. http://www.ala.org/acrl/sites/ala.org.acrl/files/content/conferences/confsandpreconfs/national/2011/papers/hanging_together.pdf.

McClure, Randall, and James P. Purdy, eds. *The Future Scholar: Researching & Teaching the Frameworks for Writing and Information Literacy*. Medford, NJ: Information Today, 2016.

McGuinness, Claire. "What Faculty Think—Exploring the Barriers to Information Literacy Development in Undergraduate Education." *The Journal of Academic Librarianship* 32, no. 6 (2006): 573–82.

Mead, George H. "A Behavioristic Account of the Significant Symbol." *The Journal of Philosophy* 19, 1922, 157–63.

Meulemans, Yvonne Nalani, and Allison Carr. "Not at Your Service: Building Genuine Faculty-Librarian Partnerships." *Reference Services Review* 41, no. 1 (2013): 80–90. doi:10.1108/00907321311300893.

Meyer, Jan, Ray Land, and Caroline Baillie, eds. *Threshold Concepts and Transformational Learning.* Educational Futures: Rethinking Theory and Practice, 42. Rotterdam: Sense Publishers, 2010.

Mirtz, Ruth. "Encountering Library Databases: Nextgen Students' Strategies for Reconciling Personal Topics and Academic Scholarship." In *The New Digital Scholar: Exploring and Enriching the Research and Writing Practices of NextGen Students*, edited by Randall McClure and James P. Purdy, 189–207. ASIS&T Monograph Series. Medford, NJ: Information Today, 2013.

Mounce, M. "Academic Librarian and English Composition Instructor Collaboration: A Selective Annotated Bibliography 1998-2007." *Reference Services Review* 37, no. 1 (2009): 44–53. doi:10.1108/00907320910934986.

National Research Council (U.S.), John Bransford, James W. Pellegrino, and Suzanne Donovan. *How People Learn: Brain, Mind, Experience, and School.* Expanded ed. Washington, D.C: National Academies Press, 2000.

Nelson, Jennie. *"This Was an Easy Assignment": Examining How Students Interpret Academic Writing Tasks.* Technical Report, 43. Berkeley, CA: Center for the Study of Writing, 1990.

Nelson, Jennie, and John R. Hayes. *How the Writing Context Shapes College Students' Strategies for Writing from Sources.* Technical Report, 16. Berkeley, CA: Center for the Study of Writing, 1988.

Norgaard, Rolf. "Writing Information Literacy: Contributions to a Concept." *Reference & User Services Quarterly* 43, no. 2 (Winter 2003): 124–30.

———. "Writing Information Literacy in the Classroom: Pedagogical Enactments and Implications." *Reference User Services Quarterly* 43, no. 3 (2004): 220–26.

O'Connor, Lisa G. "Librarians' Professional Struggles in the Information Age: A Critical Analysis of Information Literacy," 2006. PhD diss., Kent State University, 2006.

Christine Pawley. "Information Literacy: A Contradictory Coupling." *The Library Quarterly: Information, Community, Policy* 73, no. 4 (2003): 422–52. http://www.jstor.org/stable/4309685.

Perkins, David N., and Gavriel Salomon. "Transfer of Learning." Educational Leadership 46, no. 1 (1988): 22–32.

Poster, Mark. "Databases as Discourse; or, Electronic Interpellations." In *Computers, Surveillance, and Privacy*, edited by David Lyon and Elia Zureik, 175–92. Minneapolis: University of Minnesota Press, 1996.

Purdy, James P. "The Changing Space of Research: Web 2.0 and the Integration of Research and Writing Environments." *Computers and Composition* 27, no. 1 (2010): 48–58.

Purdy, James P., and Joyce R. Walker. "Liminal Spaces and Research Identity: The Construction of Introductory Composition Students as Researchers." *Pedagogy: Critical Approaches to Teaching Literature, Language, Composition, and Culture* 13, no. 1 (Winter 2013): 9–41.

Rabinowitz, Celia. "Working in a Vacuum: A Study of the Literature of Student Research and Writing." *Research Strategies* 17, no. 4 (2000): 337–46. doi:10.1016/S0734-3310(01)00052-0.

Robinson, Tracy Ann, and Vicki Tolar Burton. "The Writer's Personal Profile: Student Self Assessment and Goal Setting at Start of Term." *Across the Disciplines: Interdisciplinary Perspectives on Language, Learning, and Academic Writing* 6, Special Issue: WAC and Assessment (2009). http://wac.colostate.edu/atd/assessment/robinson_burton.cfm.

Rogers, Paul. "The Contributions of North American Longitudinal Studies of Writing in Higher Education to Our Understanding of Writing Development." In *Traditions of Writing Research*, edited by Charles Bazerman, Robert Krut, Karen

Lunsford, Susan McLeod, Suzie Null, Paul Rogers, and Amanda Stansell, 365–77. New York; London: Routledge, 2010.

Rogers, Priscilla S., and Song Mei Lee-Wong. "Reconceptualizing Politeness to Accommodate Dynamic Tensions in Subordinate-to-Superior Reporting." *Journal of Business and Technical Communication* 17, no. 4 (October 2003): 379–412.

Rose, Mike. "The Language of Exclusion: Writing Instruction at the University." *College English* 47, no. 4 (1985): 341–359.

Russell, David R. "The Writing-Across-the-Curriculum Movement: 1970-1990." In *Writing Across the Curriculum: A Critical Sourcebook*, edited by Terry Myers Zawacki and Paul M. Rogers, 15–45. Bedford/St. Martin's Series in Rhetoric and Composition. Boston: Bedford/St. Martins, 2012.

———.*Writing in the Academic Disciplines: A Curricular History*. 2nd ed. Carbondale: Southern Illinois University Press, 2002.

Saunders, Laura. "Faculty Perspectives on Information Literacy as a Student Learning Outcome." *Journal of Academic Librarianship* 38, no. 4 (July 2012): 226–36. doi:10.1016/j.acalib.2012.06.001.

Schell, Eileen E. *Gypsy Academics and Mother-Teachers: Gender, Contingent Labor, and Writing Instruction*. CrossCurrents. Portsmouth, NH: Boynton/Cook Publishers, 1998.

Schroeder, Robert. *Critical Journeys: How 14 Librarians Came to Embrace Critical Practice*. Sacramento, CA: Library Juice Press, 2014.

Schwegler, Robert A., and Linda K. Shamoon. "The Aims and Process of the Research Paper." *College English* 44, no.8 (1982): 817–824.

Seale, Maura. "The Neoliberal Library." In *Information Literacy and Social Justice: Radical Professional Praxis*, edited by Lua Gregory and Shana Higgins, 39–61. Sacramento, CA: Library Juice Press, 2013.

Sheils, Merrill. "Why Johnny Can't Write." *Newsweek* 92, no. 8 (1975): 58–65.

Sheridan, Jean, ed. *Writing-Across-the-Curriculum and the Academic Library: A Guide for Librarians, Instructors, and Writing Program Directors.* Westport, CT: Greenwood Press, 1995.

Sommers, Nancy, and Laura Saltz. "The Novice as Expert: Writing the Freshman Year." *College Composition and Communication* 56, no. 1 (2004): 124–49.

Stenberg, Shari, and Amy Lee. "Developing Pedagogies: Learning the Teaching of English." *College English* 64, no. 3 (2002): 326–47.

Thompson, Gordon W. "Faculty Recalcitrance about Bibliographic Instruction." *Bibliographic Instruction in Practice*, January 1993, 103–5.

Thompson, Gordon W. "Faculty Recalcitrance about Bibliographic Instruction." In *Bibliographic Instruction in Practice: A Tribute to the Legacy of Evan Farber*, edited by Larry L. Hardesty, Jamie Hastreiter, and David Henderson, 103–105. Library Orientation Series, 24. Ann Arbor, MI: Pierian Press, 1993.

Townsend, Martha. "WAC Program Vulnerability and What to Do About It." In *Writing Across the Curriculum : A Critical Sourcebook*, edited by Terry Myers Zawacki and Paul M. Rogers, 543–56. Bedford/St. Martin's Series in Rhetoric and Compostition. Boston: Bedford/St. Martins, 2012.

Valentine, Barbara. "The Legitimate Effort in Research Papers: Student Commitment versus Faculty Expectations." *Journal of Academic Librarianship* 27, no. 2 (March 2001): 107–115.

Veach, Grace L. "Tracing Boundaries, Effacing Boundaries: Information Literacy as an Academic Discipline." PhD diss., University of Southern Florida, 2012. http://scholarcommons.usf.edu/cgi/viewcontent.cgi?article=5609&context=etd.

Vye, Nancy J., Susan R. Goldman, James F. Voss, Cindy Hmelo, and Susan Williams. "Complex Mathematical Problem Solving by Individuals and Dyads." *Cognition and Instruction* 15, no. 4 (1997): 435–84.

Walter, Scott. "Librarians as Teachers: A Qualitative Inquiry into Professional Identity." *College & Research Libraries* 69, no. 1 (January 2008): 51–71.

Wiggins, Grant P., and Jay McTighe. *Understanding by Design.* Alexandria, VA: Association for Supervision and Curriculum Development, 1998.

Wilson, Pauline. "Librarians as Teachers: The Study of an Organization Fiction." *Library Quarterly* 49, no. 2 (1979): 146–62.

Witek, Donna, and Teresa Grettano. "Revising for Metaliteracy: Flexible Course Design to Support Social Media Pedagogy." In *Metaliteracy in Practice*, edited by Trudi E. Jacobson and Thomas P. Mackey, 1–22. Chicago: Neal-Schuman Publishers, 2015.

———. "Teaching Metaliteracy: A New Paradigm in Action." *Reference Services Review* 42, no. 2 (2014): 188–208.

Writing in the Disciplines Program, University of Vermont. "Writing & Information Literacy in the Disciplines (WILD)," 2016. https://www.uvm.edu/wid/?Page=partners.html.

Yancey, Kathleen Blake, Liane Robertson, and Kara Taczak. *Writing Across Contexts: Transfer, Composition, and Sites of Writing.* Logan: Utah State University Press, 2014.

Zurkowski, Paul G. *The Information Service Environment Relationships and Priorities.* Related Paper No.5. Washington, DC: National Commission on Libraries and Information Science, National Program for Library and Information Services, 1974.

# INDEX

CPSIA information can be obtained
at www.ICGtesting.com
Printed in the USA
BVOW04s0006071216
470014BV00002B/2/P